June

May this stimulate
you into your roots

Bill Nein

Bon Voyage

on your journey!

Anne
Nein

You Can't Grow Up
· TILL ·
You Go Back Home

⅋

You Can't Grow Up

· *TILL* ·

You Go Back Home

A Safe Journey
to See Your Parents as Human

❧

WILLIAM NERIN

CROSSROAD · NEW YORK

1993

The Crossroad Publishing Company
370 Lexington Avenue, New York, NY 10017

Copyright © 1993 by William Nerin

Printed in the United States of America

Library of Congress Cataloging-in-Publication Data
Nerin, William F.
    You can't grow up till you go back home : a safe journey to see
your parents as human / William Nerin.
        p. cm.
    ISBN 0-8245-1225-1
    1. Parent and child—United States. I. Title.
HQ755.86.N47   1993
306.874—dc20   92-42915
                                                              CIP

Musing

∽

IT'S 9:15 P.M., Crested Butte, Colo. I'm lying in my bed, reading. I'm distracted by two voices beneath the window. A young woman and a young man, strangers, are getting acquainted, making a human connection.

A few sentences about their bikes — then the most conversationally common and most unwittingly profound question escapes her lips: "Where are you from?"

"Where are you from?" comes before "What's your name?"

What is so profound about the sequence of these two questions is not what the immediate information might bring to the woman — "I'm from Tallahassee"/"Joe Schneider" — but it betrays a profound truth about life: *If I find out where you come from, your source of life, your roots, I'll know who you are.*

These two questions, in the brief encounter, sum up a central pursuit, an abiding inquiry of life itself. I want to know who I am, to discover myself. Discovering my roots, my source, where I'm from, will tell me who I am.

Contents

Appreciation

ᔥ

SOMETIMES AN AUTHOR dedicates a book to someone or something. It seems to me that the very writing of this book and getting it published demanded a dedication. So if there is any sort of dedication, it is my dedication to the ideas expressed in this book. I am dedicated to getting this book into many hands with the hope that what I have written can be of some help to others.

However, as I think about what I have done in writing this book, I am aware of feeling a deep sense of appreciation. I appreciate and honor my roots. I honor Edward Rodier and Cordelia LaGarde from Quebec, Canada, who gave life to seven children after they met and married in Kansas. Their second child was Corinne, who became my mother. I honor Corinne and her brothers and sisters, especially Jo, who became my favorite aunt and adult friend before she died in 1947.

I honor John Nearin, born in 1855 in County Sligo, Ireland, and Mary Ellen O'Keefe, born in 1860 in County Kilkenny, Ireland. They were married and had four children in Cincinnati, Ohio, one dying in childbirth. The second oldest, Bill, became my father. I honor Bill and his siblings. Unfortunately I set eyes only on Mary Ellen, Bill, and Nell. The others were dead by the time I came along.

I honor the French Canadian strain of blood and culture and the Irish background of my roots. I honor their Catholicism as giving me certain values.

I honor Celeste and Norvell, the children my mother had prior to her marriage with Bill. While they were my half sister and brother, we were so close that I have never considered them as any other than my sister and brother. As I grew up they became my respected friends as we continued to open our hearts to each other.

As I write this, I feel a sadness within me. All these people have left this plane of existence. I miss them in a way, yet feel filled by them at this very moment. As I look back upon my life with them, I see that I wouldn't have wanted it any different. Even the pain and hurt I experienced in growing up challenged me to be who and what I am. I thank them for what they have given to me.

I also wish to thank all those friends of mine who have been kind enough to read and criticize parts of this book, to give me helpful suggestions and mostly to be "with me" in this endeavor.

To each and every one of you, I say, "Thanks."

However, the one sustaining friend, without whom I doubt I would have completed this work, is my wife, Anne. She has stood by me in my ups and downs, encouraging me, being patient with me, and believing in me. An amateur editor and professional therapist, she has read every word, offering me literary and professional suggestions as the chapters unfolded. Her views gave me additional confidence in what I was doing.

A Personal Statement

❦

AS I LOOK BACK ON MY LIFE, I am amazed how often I have made important life decisions or embarked upon a serious course of action based on factors only partially known to me at the time. Years later I discover other reasons that may have been far more important for me than those I had at the time.

Today, I am convinced that I gravitated toward the field of family therapy and toward one of the world's leading family therapists, Virginia Satir, and a process she invented called family reconstruction because of forces within me that I was not aware of at the time.

One of these unconscious factors was to attend to some family matters of my own that I did not think were of concern to me when I embarked upon these activities.

I grew up during the Depression in the 1930s. Separated for a time from my parents and living with my maternal grandparents, I learned to be very self-sufficient, independent, and resourceful. I was highly moral and considered by others, and later on by myself, to be a very good boy. During these early years I absorbed a great deal of pain, which I thought little of. It was just part of normal life. Our family and my parents' families were terrific survivors. They took the hits and went on. Both families saw life as an adventure that was worth the risks and that brought rewards and, at times, great suffering.

1

Human beings, family, and relating to one another were the important elements of life, not careers or accumulating money and power.

The pain I experienced came from the hardships of the Depression — my parents falling apart, my father's alcoholism, my parents arguing, and all the low self-esteem my father felt because he could not recover from his illness. My personal pain, however, was experienced in an environment of an extended family that would hang in there to protect the family members. I grew up watching how the extended family took care of each other. One of the delightful stories told was how the Rodier kids (my mother's family of seven children) would fight among themselves, but heaven help the kids who would attack a Rodier. The Rodiers stuck together to protect their own.

So in spite of all the anguish (which at times became somatic; once I became crippled for no reason except allergies!) I felt I would *always be taken care of.*

While I forged ahead with my schooling and young adult life, I put the pain behind me, or so I thought. I was not aware how much embarrassment and shame was in me about my father and the chaotic relationship between him and my mother. I was not aware of what the fear of his uncontrolled drinking was doing to the relationship between him and me.

I coped with it by growing distant from my father and protecting myself from future pain by not getting seriously involved with others. That is, if I kept a certain detachment, even though a person left me or a relationship failed, I would not be severely hurt. I could become enormously caring and connected to people I helped in therapy for the hour or months I was with them because I knew there was no permanent commitment. My pain had developed my capacity to care for and fully feel with others, a positive gain, but it also kept me from plunging into an all-or-nothing relationship.

Left with one very competent and powerful parent, my mother, without the balance of an equally functioning father, I also kept a certain distance from her for many years. I was afraid of being taken over by her.

So in a very real sense, to protect myself I kept a healthy distance between myself and my parents. I was always pleasantly present to them in need or on those special family gathering days.

I was kind and thoughtful to them. But I kept my emotional distance

What I was doing was both positive and negative. On the positive side, I was protecting myself, through my distance, from being dominated or suffering pain. On the negative side, I was cut off from my roots. I was, in effect, not very rooted or grounded.

As I became engaged in the studies of human nature, human motivation, psychology, and family dynamics, I began better to understand myself as well as my parents. Then I learned the family reconstruction process from Virginia Satir. I discuss this process in chapters 18, 19, and 20.

So my venture into psychology, family therapy, and family reconstruction allowed me slowly to close the distance between me and my parents. Conversations with my mother in the 1960s and 1970s closed most of the emotional distance between her and me. My father had died in 1960.

It was from guiding family reconstructions, which I began in 1975, and in doing my own soon after that I began to heal the wounds between me and my father. Let me give you a few examples.

When I prepared the genogram, or family tree, of my father's family, I put together for the first time on one piece of paper the fact that my father had experienced three deaths in his family. When my father was two years old, he lost a baby brother during childbirth; when he was ten, his older sister, Mayme, who was twelve, was killed in a street-car accident; and when he was sixteen, his father died at the age of forty-five.

Seeing these three deaths outlined on the paper in front of me produced a reaction of surprise more that anything else.

My overall perception of my father included, among other things, seeing him as happy-go-lucky with a live-and-let-live-spirit, but not very responsible or serious. Early on, I remembered arguments between my mother and father when my mother would scold my father for not saving money for the future.

Doing his genogram* did not change this perception. It was during my family reconstruction several years later that the perception began to change.

---

*Genogram is a way of drawing the family tree that records vital information so that the viewer can understand possible relationships and dynamics within the family. See p. 96 for an example.

During this reconstruction each of these deaths was reenacted. After the death of my father's father, when my father was sixteen years old, the Guide of the reconstruction turned to the person playing the role of my father and asked, "What's going on with you?"

The role player turned and with a slow, sad voice said, "I've made a decision: Live each day to the fullest. You never know when you will die."

As the scenes unfolded, I saw my father quitting school and getting a full-time job to support the family; he was the oldest child and had a younger sister, Nell, nine years old.

Days after the family reconstruction, I began to appreciate for the first time that my father had a serious and responsible side to him, that he curtailed his education and carried the responsibility of supporting the family. Was this one reason he married so late in life, when he was thirty-eight years old?

I also understood the basis of the arguments about money. Making a life decision to live each day as if it might be your last, explains the lack of interest in saving for a rainy day (which soon came in the Great Depression). I suspected that my mother never understood the genesis of this dynamic in my father.

I also began to see how deeply sensitive and caring my father was beneath his *joie de vivre* attitude. As the days and months went on it slowly dawned on me that this sensitivity would be the basis of extreme pain when he would feel rejected or like a failure. This sensitivity would make any feelings of low self-esteem sharply felt. I could understand why distractions would be an easy coping mechanism to deal with the pain. He could use his fabulous sense of humor and zest for play and fun as tools to escape pain. He could drink to deaden the pain.

So from my reconstruction I gradually shifted my perception of my father from one of a happy-go-lucky, rather irresponsible, and later sick person to that of a person who was indeed very responsible, who as youth, endured much pain, which deepened his sensitivity and feeling, who decided that each day was the day in which to live, and who suffered the pain of his adult life in a way I had no idea of.

Then the great awakening! He is like me; I am like him! I gradually, within myself, began shifting from being his little boy to being on an equal basis with him. I felt as big as he. I grew up inside. I began to be appropriately connected to him in the 1980s, twenty years after he had died. I could abandon the distance I had created with him. I could at last begin to accept and affirm him as part of me, my roots. I made enormous progress in my own personal and spiritual growth and maturation.

In 1982, after being single my entire life, I ventured into a serious, life-long, committed relationship. I married Anne. The journey of achieving deeper intimacy is ongoing. We are never finished.

And now I invite you to read the following pages, to consider how they might apply to you, and to react to what I am presenting. This book is a compilation of stories, ideas, and suggestions taken from my experience in learning from people through doing family therapy, especially family reconstruction.

THE PEOPLE DESCRIBED IN THESE PAGES are real in the sense that they are descriptive of many of the people I have encountered in my professional life, especially those who have gained a new appreciation of their family roots. They are fictional in the sense that details have been altered to disguise their real identities. While the story lines are fictional, the reality imbedded in the fiction is true.

In these pages I speak with certain convictions that come mainly from my own experience. I present no research that definitively proves my thesis and my views. Neither my convictions nor the lack of research are of paramount importance. What is important is that you, the reader, trust your own sense and form your own judgment as to the possible validity of the views presented here. If you think there is value in what I am proposing then you may be motivated to begin or continue on with the great adventure of rerooting with your family.

Chapter One

What This Book Is About

❧

A THIRTY-FIVE-YEAR-OLD MAN wrote this letter to his dad. I have excerpted parts of it, but the essence remains.

Dear Dad,

Believe it or not, I have been wanting to write this letter for more than ten years, but doing so has never been as important to me as it is now. I have so much pain that I have never shared with you. I need to let it go. I need to let you know who I am.

I have only recently realized that I have been living my life as if by script, with very few feelings or emotions surfacing. I have never felt good enough to express my real self: my thoughts, feelings, aspirations, and even my negative "stuff." I have lived behind a façade for a long time.

Starting from a young age, I learned to either hide or medicate my feelings with drugs and alcohol. I was afraid to be who I was. I didn't like myself. Somehow, I felt responsible for you and mom divorcing.

I wanted so badly to share my pain with someone but was afraid of the consequences. I felt like there was no one I could turn to. Most of my feelings were turned inward and against myself. I have presented a wonderful façade of togetherness throughout my life. The reality is, however, that I haven't felt very good about me. For me, the process of changing this image is by sharing it with two of the most significant people in my life, my parents. [He wrote a separate letter to his mother.]

As I mentioned earlier, I used drugs and alcohol to hide from really expressing myself. While I don't use the drugs or alcohol anymore, the walls I created to protect myself are still there.

I've also realized that we don't really know each other. Our relationship has been kept at an emotional distance. It's strange, but I have very few childhood memories of us interacting.

I have often thought how difficult it must have been for you to raise us kids. This was such a big responsibility, especially since we were in our formative years. I thank you for doing your best. I know you never meant to hurt me. *Unfortunately, I judged you negatively for so many years. My judgments are beginning to change and are being replaced with love and understanding.*

I wish you could see the person I am becoming. I am unfolding into a loving, caring, concerned human being. The process is slow for me, but it is working. I am beginning to feel "good enough" about myself, and I see I can make a positive difference in the world. I am also an emotional person full of feelings and empathy. I am learning to express this and be who I really am.

Dad, I am growing up. I am loving myself. Thank you for bringing me into the world. I love you. I know you love me too. Showing it has been hard for us.

Love,
Jason

This letter, from which I quoted a few passages, is powerful and emotional. It took great courage for Jason to write it. What gave him the courage to do so, risking possible rejection? Why would he write it?

I think of three elements that provide the answer. First, this thirty-five-year-old man, being at odds with and separated from his parents, feels a need to heal that separation. Being separated, he feels incomplete. He is not whole because he is cut off from his roots. There is a terribly strong need for human beings to feel whole, complete. When that wholeness is absent, a person feels emptiness on some level. This man was able to let that feeling of emptiness enter into his full awareness. He was able to feel that emptiness in all its anguish. Thus he felt the overwhelming urge to do something about it.

The second element is that Jason in some way had come to understand that the two people to whom he was appealing were human beings before they were parents. Consequently, he was able to relate to them in his heart and mind, not on the basis of the roles they had played in his life, but as the people they are, prior to becoming a mother and a father. He was beginning to understand them as being human as he is human. Thus he could see them as vulnerable, fearful, doubtful, lacking confidence and power, confused. He was shifting his perception of them as parents with the parental qualities of being stronger, smarter, more assured, more capable than he was. This is indicated when Jason said, "I have often thought how difficult it must have been for you to raise us kids. This was such a big responsibility, especially since we were in our formative years."

Seeing them as human as he was, he saw them more as his equals rather than as in a down-up position with them based on the child-parent relationship. Thus he felt less intimidated by their position and power as parents. Seeing them as human also gave him some confidence that he could reach them on that basis of their *shared humanity*. This emerging feeling of equality and confidence is the second element that encouraged him to write his letter.

The third element flows from the second. Sensing his own adulthood, *feeling* like an adult, he now could handle their possible rejection in a far better way than he could as a child. A child is devastated by rejection because the helpless child *needs* the parent to survive. The adult is not so devastated because the adult can survive without the parent. So the thirty-five-year-old Jason was realizing on some level that he would not be destroyed if his letter met with disapproval, which might result in his being hurt. He could now handle that hurt and get on with his life, even though he would still feel the emptiness of being separated from his roots in the day-to-day relationship with his parents. (I must add that most thirty-five-year-old men and women know intellectually that they are adults. What is amazing is how many don't feel that adulthood when they are with their parents. They emotionally see their parents differently than other adults of their age.)

The wonderful thing about this story is that the parents responded with understanding, love, and affection to Jason's letter. In fact Jason saw his father cry for the first time in his life! This only deepened the emotional conviction that his father was indeed as human as he is. This opened the door for Jason to accept his father and mother as human, part of his roots, part of himself. The emptiness was filled, the separation healed. The thirty-five-year-old man felt whole and confident and enjoyed greater self-esteem. Jason wrote the following to me. "Our relationship has greatly improved since sending my father the letter. We are communicating much more than in the past. I actually look forward to seeing him and spending time with him. That's a first!"

Not everyone who risks as Jason did has the same outcome. Some are rebuffed by their parents. However, even if the day-to-day relationship is not healed, there is a way whereby a person can accept one's roots at least within the intimacy of one's heart.

People, if they are willing, *can* reconnect with their family roots in a way that is *new,* safe, relieving, joyous, and productive. This provides a light-hearted spirit, a greater sense of one's identity, and a self-worth that allows one to be strong and confident in facing life.

This journey to accept or deepen the acceptance of one's roots, especially one's parents, is what this book is all about. This book explains the essential key to achieve this goal, a key many overlook. It is because this key is missed that so many fail to embrace their roots as part of themselves and thus remain incomplete.

This book also explains why some resist embarking upon this journey. For those who are willing to take the journey, this book describes various ways that this can be accomplished. It offers specific plans and tasks.

This book will appeal to those who feel cut off in some way from their parents and roots. It will appeal to those desiring to advance their human and spiritual lives by becoming more rooted, completing the circle, as it were. It will attract those entering into late adulthood and who are beginning to discover stirrings to go back home again to deepen their connection with their origins.

In fact, this rerooting, or completing the circle, may be the final stage in personality development, as important as the stage of adolescence. It is my belief that being grounded in one's roots is also an important step to preparing oneself to face death with peace.

Chapter Two

The New Way
of Reconnecting to Roots

❧

ONE DAY FRED, a friend of mine, asked me what I'd been up to recently. I told him I was working on a new book. "What is it about?" he asked. I told him that the theme of the book was about the need for people to relate to their parents in a way that is different from the old way of relating to them as parents.

"What do you mean?" he said.

"Well, Fred, we have spent the most impressionable years of our life — from birth to eighteen — in perceiving our parents as parents. As we become adults it is important to begin to see them differently, that is, as human beings just like us. We need to feel that we are as adult as they are, that we are on an equal basis with them. We need to begin to see them as respected friends rather than as protectors and caretakers."

He paused a bit, then laughed, almost snickered I thought, and said, "I don't see anything new in that. All of us are adults. How else are we going to relate to our parents except as we are. I know they are human. What else are they?"

I felt stuck. Had Fred really understood what I was talking about? Yes, we are adults, but does that mean that we relate to our parents as equals? So many of us don't.

Or had Fred really accomplished what I had in mind? Had he shifted his perception of his parents in such a way that he related

THE NEW WAY OF RECONNECTING TO ROOTS

to his parents as fellow human beings? Did he really *feel* equal to them? Did he *feel* as big as they are? And if he did, did this allow him to accept them as they are with all their lovable and unlovable traits? Did he accept them without necessarily needing to change them for his sake or self-esteem? Did this acceptance remove from him any need to deny or ignore part of his roots? Did Fred actually embrace his parents and relatives as part of himself? Was he psychologically one with his root system? Did he feel complete and whole? Did this completion allow Fred the freedom and strength to protect himself from his parents if they might still hurt him at times?

Perhaps Fred is like many who do shift their perceptions of their parents as they grow up. They do see them more as humans and less as godlike parents. They enter into a comfortable, easygoing relationship with them. They become friends and confidants with their parents. They can swap stories of their lives, dreams, disappointments, successes, and failures. They can, without threat, tell each other how in the past they hurt each other, or got angry, or worried about the other. They can commiserate with each other over their failures without feeling the need to lecture each other. They can confront each other without feeling guilt. They can be honest with each other without fearing the loss of approval because they are secure in themselves, not needing that approval for their own self-worth. They are easy with each other because they no longer need to try to change the other.

Perhaps Fred has achieved that with his mother and father. If he has, I know that Fred has an edge on many, that he has a strength and well-being that others are missing. Fred has rounded himself out through the years, he has come full circle, he has fully connected in a loving and accepting way with his roots. He is whole. Thus he exudes a peace, security, confidence, and wisdom in facing life and death.

There is a way to know whether or not Fred has achieved this radical shift in perception. While with his parents, does he act the same with them as with any other adult or close friend? If so, then the chances are that the shift has occurred. If, on the other hand, he finds that he acts differently when at home than with other adults, there is a good chance that the shift has not occurred. For example, does he guard his words, is he afraid of their disapproval? An even better test, however, is, does he feel younger or smaller in their presence than he does in the presence of others the age of his parents?

Another way to test whether the shift has occurred is to see how comfortable we are with *thinking* of our parents as "Cecil and Jane" rather than as "father and mother." (It may be uncomfortable actually to use the first names because of habit or because the parents feel ill at ease.) Words are powerful symbols. Having used the symbols "father" and "mother," which refer to roles that Cecil and Jane have played, it is usually difficult for us to use new symbols that refer to them as persons. If we do see them now primarily in their personhood rather than in their roles it becomes easier to think and even perhaps to refer to them by their proper names.

Fred represents many who think they have a full human connection with their parents. Some do have this adult-to-adult relationship. Many still have a son/daughter-to-parent relationship.

Chapter Three

The Key
to the New Reconnecting

୬

AS A FAMILY THERAPIST, I have devoted a major portion of my work toward helping people deal with family-of-origin issues. In this work I have learned much from my respected teacher and trusted friend, the late Virginia Satir. She is one of the pioneers in the field of family therapy, which began around 1950. Satir understood what all therapists know, namely, that many, if not most, of our problems originate in our early childhood.

At the time she began her professional career as a therapist, the major thrust of psychotherapy was that of Freud. Freud discovered that he could help his patients by unveiling events and meanings hidden in a person's unconscious. Once the person became aware of that which was hidden, and got an insight into what was going on, then the person would heal. Insight therapy works for many people.

When that type of therapy didn't work for Satir, she began experimenting with other approaches. In her explorations, she discovered that many people's problems, especially those caused by early family experiences, could be solved *only* if the clients could accept their parents and other significant members of their family of origin *as part of themselves*. She began to realize that when we must look down upon, reject, disown, or ignore, a vital part of ourselves, that leads to low self-worth. And our roots are a vital part of ourselves. Therefore, as long as we are disconnected in any way from our roots, our self-worth is in jeopardy.

When we feel bad about ourselves, we have little energy or confidence and fewer resources to get on in life. So Satir saw that she had to help people feel better about themselves by being able to accept all of their parts — including their roots.

Well enough, but how do you help a person accept a mother or father who has caused great pain in that person's life? How can a person be willing to embrace as part of himself or herself a father who abandoned the family, or a mother who was a tyrant? How can a person be accepting of a physically or sexually abusing parent? How can a person relate to a person who for all intents and purposes was never there — as with an adopted person? How can a person get over anger toward a parent who placed undue burdens on the person as a child, for example, by demanding perfection, by manipulating the child to make the parent happy, by demanding that the child be the exact replica of the parent, by expecting the child to take the place of the dead sibling or of the boy or girl who never was in the family?

What is the *key* to being able to accept one's roots? What is the key that allows a person to reconnect with parents, grandparents, aunts, and uncles in the new way described in the last chapter, that is, to see them as human rather than in their roles? The key is what Satir saw and what I have seen over the years as a therapist. *The key is to take a person back to the families his or her mother and father grew up in.* The key is not to deal only with the immediate family the person was raised in, which is what much family of origin work tends to do. The key to changing a person's vision of parents from that of mother and father to that of Jane and Cecil is to let the person understand what is was like for Jane and Cecil to be born, to learn to walk, talk, use the toilet, go to school. It is to help the person see what scared Cecil and Jane as children, what dreams they had, what they wanted to be when grown. It is to help the person understand what Cecil and Jane liked and disliked in their parents. It is to help the person see what pain and happiness Jane and Cecil experienced in their homes, what successes and failures were theirs while growing up. It is to enable the person to see what needs were satisfied and what needs were never met in Jane and Cecil's lives. It is to aid the person to see what Cecil and Jane learned about what it is to be a man, woman, husband, wife, father, mother. It is to help the person see the impact on Jane and Cecil's lives from deaths that occurred in the families when they were small.

The key is to help the person see Cecil and Jane's awkwardness going through puberty, to see them attracted to the opposite sex, to see them dating, getting engaged and married. It is to allow the person to realize what went on in the minds and hearts of Jane and Cecil when they discovered they were pregnant, what their reactions were at his or her birth.

We have never seen these things first hand because when we are born we meet our parents fully grown with all these experiences behind them. Thus it is hard to realize that our parents flirted, smooched, became sexually aroused with each other; it is hard to realize that these parents were once vulnerable, dependent children as we were. What makes this realization even more difficult is that parents tend to hide their vulnerabilities and reveal only godlike qualities such as omniscience and omnipotence.

Once we can go back, in the many ways I'll describe later on, to the early lives of our mother and father, then it is possible to see them as persons just "like me." It is being able to see them as red-blooded human beings who dream dreams, suffer hurts and misunderstandings, want approval and acceptance, tremble with hidden fears, exude or suppress sexual energy, aspire to the ideal while feeling less than ideal.

Going back to the paternal and maternal families is the key to seeing them as human. And when we perceive them, in our guts, as human we can then accept them as part of us. When we can accept our roots as part of us, our self-esteem rises, our personal resources become available to us, and our personal boundaries can expand.

Chapter Four

"Don't Tell Me
I Have to Go Home Again!"

♋

"HISTORY IS HISTORY; the past is gone and forgotten; it's what's here now that counts; the issue is to move on in life." This expresses the view of countless people. On the other hand, many cultures and religions and a vast body of the world's literature claim that honoring and accepting one's roots is exactly what makes the here and now count and allows one to get on in life. As Ken Burns, the film maker of the PBS series on the Civil War, claims, the past illuminates the present, and history is not who we were, it's who we are.

So why is there such a reluctance on the part of so many to take the trip back home again? In my practice I have encountered several reasons explaining this reluctance.

The one that I think is the most profound as well as most hidden is a deep-seated fear of losing one's self-identity. Let me explain this in the context of my experience as a therapist.

One of the ways of completing the circle, of rerooting with one's family on an adult-to-adult level, is through a process called family reconstruction. There is a chapter on this process later in the book.

One of the steps in this process is a day-long event that takes place within a group in which trust and cohesion have been developed. During the day, the Explorer, the one doing the recon-

18

necting, chooses persons from the group to play the members of his or her paternal and maternal families and the family of origin. Critical scenes in the history of the three families are reenacted using drama and pantomime and placing role players in various physical positions as if in a sculpture. The most common scenes reenacted are births, deaths, dating and engagement, marriages, illnesses, financial successes and reversals, family moves and going to war, as well as typical scenes such as the family dinner, Christmas celebration, and coming home with a report card.

As a result of the day's activity, the Explorer has the opportunity to revisit his or her family lineage in order to see these family members in a deeper, different, and more human way.

On one occasion when I was guiding a family reconstruction, one of the group members invited a friend, Susie, to witness the process. Susie was intrigued and on some level understood the implications of what she saw. When the day was over, she told me she found family reconstruction fascinating and asked if she could visit another session. At the same time she declared loudly and clearly: "Bill, don't get the idea that I want to do this. No way. I've got my folks exactly where I want them. I have spent years getting them to where I can handle them and I'm not going to disturb that at all. My life is just fine as it is!"

What is behind such a strong stand? Susie obviously saw the possibility of a new way of being with her folks. On that day she saw how it changed the way her friend viewed and felt about his parents. When she returned for her second visit, she was still adamant. "I see my folks as they are, and I don't want to change that."

What was so threatening to Susie? Why did she not want to tamper with the way she viewed, felt, and dealt with her parents? Let me try to explain.

When Susie, you, and I came into this world, we were helpless and vulnerable. To survive physically and psychologically, we had to depend on our parents (or substitute parents). Our maturation as humans takes longer than that of any other creature in the animal kingdom, so we spend more time depending on our parents. Because we are dependent for so long, our ties and bonds with them are extremely strong. Our parents are an integral part of us. We are one with our roots.

Within the context of this strong bonding something very

powerful takes place. To describe this, I will use myself as an example. Since I needed my parents to survive, early on I began to do what I could to get them to like me, to love me. I could not afford to alienate them, for who else would care for me? This effort was motivated by an unconscious, instinctive drive. As I grew older I became conscious of their needs, moods, and desires and the devices I needed to employ to keep them happy with me.

I learned to imitate them, which also pleased them. I began to notice that they walked on two legs. My body was developing muscles that allowed me to walk too. They spoke words, not just noises, so as my facial muscles and mind developed I tried to speak also. When I first said "Ma, Ma," they smiled at me.

In this effort to keep them happy with me, I became obedient. I assented to all they told me. When they pointed to my nose and said, "Nose," I said, "Nose." When they pointed to the big fat animal in the field and said, "Cow," I said, "Cow."

I also learned to avoid what they disapproved of. If I did do something that they did not approve of, I noticed their voices changing from a cooing to a sharpness. Frowns appeared on their faces. Ugliness replaced pleasant smiles.

I quickly noticed that my parents were bigger, more powerful, more competent than I was. I began to notice that they did not spill their food or drop their milk! They were safe to be with. I obeyed, pleased, imitated, and became like them, and I was awarded with love and approval and their caring for me. As a result I survived.

Physical survival was not all. As I developed I began to wonder about myself, again more unconsciously than consciously. What am I? Who am I? Do I count? Am I important? Am I lovable? Am I worth anything? Yes I am — because my parents like me, enjoy me, smile at me, brag about me to others, tell my brother and sister to watch over me. I am lovable because they scoop me up and hug me, kiss me, cuddle me. I am important because they spend so much time caring for me. They rush in to meet my needs of hunger, cleanliness, and health.

I must count because my parents try to understand me. When I hurt, they comfort me. When I fear, they assure me. When I am confused, they enlighten me.

On the other hand, sometimes I get the message that I am not so important or worthwhile. I hear my parents and my brother and sister criticize me. They tell me when I err. Sometimes that is done in such a way that I feel I must be the dumbest person in the world. (At other times, however, they tell me I'm wrong in such a way that I understand that it is normal to make mistakes and I can learn from those mistakes. Then I feel okay.)

At times my parents tell me I am a bad boy. They seem exasperated with me. Their anger scares me. Sometimes they are not there for me when I'm scared or lonely, so I fear even more. Then I doubt if I really count.

When I play with others, I do not seem to fit in. At school, I have trouble with my grades. I am told how smart my older sister and brother are. Kids make fun of my eye glasses. So, I wonder if there is something the matter with me. Again, most of these thought processes are in the unconscious. But they do produce feelings of low self-worth.

Sometimes my parents argue over me. I conclude that I cause them trouble and pain, so I cannot be very good. Other times, they fight and argue; I try to stop them. When I can't, I feel helpless. My brother picks on me and my mother sides with him, so he is more loved than I, I foolishly assume. My father loses his job; my mother worries and is afraid. I make childish conclusions: If I were not around, they would not be in so much trouble. It is the thinking of a child with an undeveloped mind.

So sometimes I get the impression from the way my folks act toward me, or between themselves, that I am indeed very important, valuable, lovable — that I do count highly. Yet, at other times I get the impression that I am not worth much, I am bad, I am not lovable. The ultimate fix I get on myself depends on how the pendulum swings. If most of the time and attention from my parents is on the side that I am lovable, then I will come out in life thinking I am basically okay. But if most of my parents' behavior seems to indicate that I am a problem or that I am flawed in some sense, then I will come out in life thinking I am basically not okay and not lovable.

Keep in mind, when I come into this world not only am I vulnerable and impressionable, but my physical and mental equipment is undeveloped. Therefore my capacity to see reality is limited. My capacity to misread things, to misinterpret what is happening, is ever present, as the examples above illustrate.

I also see things as either/or. There are no shades in between.

I can see one parent as an angel and the other as a devil, or one as very strong and the other as very weak.

As a child, I also live in a world of the gods. I am helpless, ignorant, and fallible, and my parents are powerful, perfect, right, and all-knowing. We attribute to God the qualities of being omnipresent, omniscient, omnipotent, and perfect. This is the way I experience my parents. In fact, they go to great lengths to hide from me their fears, mistakes, doubts, confusions, weaknesses, ignorance. They pretend to know all, to be able to do all, and to be all — for my sake. They want me to feel safe.

Since my parents are my creators, saviors, and protectors and the guides upon whom my very existence depends, I am utterly beholden to them. What I received from them comes from on high, as it were. These are "divine" lessons and impressions. So the basic view I have of what I am, who I am, and how lovable and valuable I am, comes from parent-gods.

So I form the sense of my identity and self-worth from how I see my parents and how they relate to me. I also form this view of myself equipped with limited capacities, so I can easily gather an impression of myself that is far from reality. This perception of "who I am," coming to me in a vulnerable and impressionable state and from parents who had "divine authority," becomes deeply imbedded in the core of my personality.

Let me return to my friend, Susie. If she changes the way she sees her parents, it will change the way she sees herself and how she feels about herself, since that self-identity was formed by the way she saw her parents as a child. For some forty years she has lived with that identity formed in early childhood. She knows herself and how to survive as that person. She has well-honed habits formed around who and what she is. To shift her identity now might mean a drastic change in her life. This seems too overwhelming to Susie even though there are aspects of her life that bother her. This fear of change overshadows any desire Susie has to feel whole, confident, and resourceful in facing life. Such wholeness could be hers if she became more rooted by embracing her parents for who they fully are. Susie represents what I think is the most basic reason many resist reconnecting to their roots in a new way.

Another case that illustrates how reluctant we can be to change our self-identity is that of Howard. Howard grew up being severely criticized by his parents. As a result, he sees himself as a failure in life.

Although angry at his parents, he at the same time hungers for their love, approval, and acceptance. His feelings toward his parents are confusing and contradictory; he vacillates between placating and hating them.

Since he sees himself as a failure, Howard feels inferior, worthless, discouraged, powerless, angry, and fearful. In order to survive, he develops a stubborn streak in reaction to the edict that "you are a failure." He uses his stubborn streak to work exceedingly hard in school, on the job, in athletics, at social events — to succeed. And he does succeed up to a point, but then for some "unknown" reason he fails! He cannot explain it; none of his friends can explain it. His parents grow only more exasperated and convey the message, "We told you so; you'll never make it."

Why does Howard continue this self-defeating pattern? He has brains, good looks, and a pleasant demeanor, yet after initially succeeding, he seems to fail at every endeavor.

The problem is that — his self-identity is that of being a failure. And unconsciously *he must maintain the identity he has of himself.* Who else can he be? He is familiar with this identity. He has learned to live with it. He is twenty-nine years old and somehow has survived. When he fails, he entices those around him to bail him out, befriend him; he gets a momentary "lift" from people responding to him in trouble. So all is not lost. In the very process of failing, he gets a certain closeness from others that, for the moment, lets him believe he may be of some value.

Many of us can commiserate with a person living in this sort of hell: the frustration of repeated failure and the despair of a negative self-image. Yet in spite of this, Howard also refused to do his family reconstruction because he too sensed the power of the process. Rather, he preferred one-on-one therapy merely to talk over his problems. He avoided changing his way of perceiving his parents, which could have resulted in a change of his self-image.

We all have an identity that we formed in early childhood. *It can be very threatening to change that image.* It is like losing our life.

This is why Howard refused to do his family reconstruction. He was like Susie. Remember Susie's words, "I've got my folks exactly where I want them; I've spent years getting them to where I can handle them, and I'm not going to disturb that at all." The old cliché applies: The devil you know is better than the devil you don't know. Susie's statement also allows her to live in a delusion. She thinks she has done something to her parents, "I've got them where I want them." In reality she has done something to herself rather than to her parents. She has kept herself in her own place. She has restricted her own movement toward growth.

As adults, if Susie and Howard began to see their parents differently, not as godlike parents, but as the limited humans they are, they *would also begin to see themselves differently.* This would break up the structured set of feelings consolidated around those early perceptions, which in turn would begin to alter the ways of coping that have allowed them to survive. These changes, however, would lead them into uncharted waters in which they do not know if they could survive. Most of this way of thinking and feeling about changing goes on in the unconscious so that Susie, for example, does not understand the depth of her statement, "I'm not going to disturb that at all."

The stories of Susie and Howard illustrate what I think is the most profound reason that many resist going home again to see their parents in a different light.

There is yet another dynamic that reinforces this fear of seeing one's parents as human. Many parents need us to be what they help create. So they have a vested interest in making sure that we maintain the early image of them as the parents they are. They are reluctant to let us see their human side. They need the parent-child relationship for themselves, even though their "child" may be fifty years old. So these parents sabotage any effort their grown children may make to see their parents as human. On the flip side of the coin, the grown child has an additional pay-off. The grown child can still feel the childlike security of depending and relying on his or her parents. If the fifty-year-old began to perceive and relate to them as equals, he or she might lose this childlike security.

Often I have heard anxiety expressed by adults when their second parent dies: "Now I've lost the one last person I could count on." It's as if a shattering blow has been dealt to one's inner security. However, often it is the death of the remaining parent that helps us perceive our parents as human. Death can reveal any unconscious dependency upon the parent. It offers the occasion for adults to face the fact that they are responsible for themselves.

It is scary business to begin the journey back home. I believe it can be taken only after we have achieved the strength of some separation and individuation. I believe it will be embarked upon by those who have either high self-esteem or those who can no longer stand the pain of low self-esteem. I understand the Susies and Howards of the world.

Chapter Five

Other Reasons
Never to Return

❧

WHILE THE FEAR OF TAMPERING with one's self-identity is the most profound reason people don't go home again, there are other more obvious fears inhibiting this journey.

The first one stems from our very psychological makeup. Every person goes through the stage of puberty or adolescence. The psychological dimension of that stage is the effort, struggle if you will, to break away from parents, home, and family, in order to claim our own unique place in life. It is the stage of finding ourselves. We spend years and expend enormous emotional energy in achieving this goal.

For some it is easier than for others. It is easier for those whose parents support the effort. It is difficult for those whose parents hinder the effort. Teenagers, then, must not only contend with the normal struggles of adolescence, but must contend with their godlike parents.

To invite such persons to begin the family reconstruction process or other processes that will lead them to understand, love, and accept their parents in a different way is frightening. "If I let them close to me they will dominate me again." "I'll lose myself again." "I've fought too hard and long for my independence." "They are too powerful and overwhelming." This fear blinds such persons from seeing that there is a distinction between avoiding parental dominance in actual day-to-day encounters, and understanding and accepting one's parents within one's heart.

Accepting one's parents does not mean letting them dominate or be abusive. Rather, accepting parents includes an understanding of why their controlling or abusive behavior is a way they cope with being threatened, and what it is that threatens them.

An example of how a parent can be threatened is Janet. She lost her first two children, one in an early illness and the second in a car accident, and is now overly protective of her third child, Marilyn. Janet's fear is so strong that the slightest desire on Marilyn's part to separate from her mother threatens her. She copes by clamping down on Marilyn. Marilyn can neither move nor be on her own; any effort to break away, be herself, is thwarted. However, once she begins to break away, to get a sense of herself, she may be able to return home again to accept her mother as part of herself. This will not be achieved unless Marilyn understands how the trauma of the death of the first two children affected her mother. This will allow Marilyn to appreciate why Janet was so controlling and overly protective. Marilyn will begin to feel compassion, which opens the door to accepting Janet as the full human she is.

Persons who have had to struggle with their parents in the effort to be themselves often protect their new-found selves by being angry at their parents or by keeping distance from them. With this protection, they have the security to get on with the task of becoming adult. So the idea of reconnecting with such a parent suggests that they might begin to feel a softness toward the parent and consequently lose their protection of anger and distance.

This is one of the reasons many fail to deal with their roots, which would lead to accepting them as part of themselves. They have simply invested too much of themselves in the effort of separating and fear doing anything that might jeopardize the gains they have made. Many stay stuck in the stage of separation and remain incomplete in their growth. They are unable to connect with their parents as adult to adult. They are unable to accept their roots as part of themselves. There is a certain incompleteness, but they may not feel it for years, if ever.

Incidentally, there is a tragic irony here. To become fully ourselves and distinct from our parents requires that we eventually reconnect with whom we are trying to separate from, namely, our parents. The reason for this is twofold.

First, we cannot be fully ourselves unless we are connected in an appropriate way to all of our self, which includes our roots.

Second, we cannot *feel* grown up until we can stand in front of our parents without feeling like a little child who belongs to them; or until we can cease using anger or distance as a way to protect ourselves from someone more powerful.

Adolescence is called by many the developmental stage of "separation and individuation." I contend that individuation is not completed until we enter another, and perhaps last, stage of development that I like to call "transformation and individuation." This developmental stage involves the process of transforming one's state from being dependent on parents for approval and acceptance to that of being the center and source of one's own approval and acceptance.

Whether or not this is a distinct stage of personality and family development is something that psychologists will debate in the years to come. I think it is because I began to see how people's lives changed, indicating a distinct growth in maturity when they finally achieved this adult-to-adult relationship with their parents. Guiding family reconstructions over the last seventeen years led me to conclude that something very powerful is at stake here. Erik Erikson, one of the most prestigious writers on personality development, lists eight distinct stages of development. In the last stage, which he names the stage of Integrity, he says that achieving this peer relationship is one of several tasks of this stage. I think it is not one of several tasks, however, but is the central task making up the core of this final stage of development.

As I got into writing this book, I began to consult with colleagues to ask if anyone else was speaking to this point. The only person referred to me was Donald Williamson, Ph.D., of Houston. In 1981 and 1982 he wrote three articles in the *Journal of Marital and Family Therapy* in which he makes the claim that moving into a peer relationship with one's parents is the last stage of personality and family life development. He developed the concept of what he called "personal authority in the family system" (PAFS), essentially defined as a synthesis of differentiation of self with emotional intimacy with members of the family of origin. We did not know each other at the time. He had been working with families and individuals for over twenty years in Houston and had come to this conclusion on his own in the late 1970s. In another part of the country I came to this conclusion in the late 1980s as I was guiding family reconstructions.

When this stage is achieved, we feel strong enough to protect ourselves with means other than distance or anger. A sense of humor and lightness in not taking parental injunctions so seriously can take the place of anger and distance. At least this can take place in our heart. Often times, the actual behavior of a parent is so abusive and unreasonable that the grown adult must maintain physical separation. In other words, the adult may not be able to lessen the way the parent is threatened that causes such bizarre behavior. The cause of the threat will be found most likely in the way the parent was raised in his or her family.

Another reason why some fail to reconnect with their roots is exemplified by Marie. She is a thirty-nine-year-old energetic and vivacious woman. She is financially secure, married with two children, and is a successful realtor. She is busy, feeling overwhelmed at times. Her financial condition allows her to hire baby sitters, take off to the mountains for skiing, and take a long yearly vacation. She lives in a highly stimulating environment with an active social life, interest in cultural affairs, and a house with all the electronic conveniences of TVs and full stereo components to distract her from her deep interior silence.

Marie has a somewhat superficial relationship with her mother, who left her in the custody of her father when she was ten. Her mother divorced to marry a man in a distant city. Over the years, while Marie visited her mother periodically, she had little or no contact with her mother's side of the family. In recent years, the contact with her mother has been more frequent due to the births of the two children, but the relationship is still superficial.

Marie does not sense any void in being so disconnected from her mother and that side of her roots. The daily rush of stimulation in Marie's life distracts her from sensing any incompleteness.

Distraction, in the sense that I am using the term, is nothing other than an expenditure of energy in a direction that may not be advantageous to our growth. As we use energy in one direction, we do not have it available to use in another direction. I believe that the direction that each of us needs to go in life is found in our deeper selves. But we need courage to go into our deeper selves. This is the reason religions and students of human growth emphasize the need for meditation, contemplation, being grounded or centered, stillness, aloneness, and prayer. These methods help us go deep into ourselves, to find our direction, to discover our deeper needs.

Marie is too busy to be still, to meditate. So she doesn't taste the sense of something missing. She is distracted.

Distraction afflicts many people. Ken Wilber has written extensively on just one aspect of the phenomenon of distracting oneself from what is essential for growth. In *The Atman Project* (Wheaton, Ill.: Quest, 1980) and later in *Up from Eden* (Boulder, Colo.: Shambhala, 1983), he gives a profound explanation and description of our efforts to deny, avoid, and distract ourselves from the fact of death. In fact, he theorizes that the history and development of human consciousness can be told from the point of view of how humankind either avoids or faces death.

The capacity to distract ourselves from what may be needed for our human growth is common. I think that the need to return home again, completing the circle, in the way I have been describing can be as challenging for some as is the challenge of facing death itself.

Another road block that keeps us from connecting with our roots is the fear of pain. I will never forget Ned, a man in his early thirties and a recovering poly-drug addict, who came to me to do his family reconstruction. He knew on some level that it was very important for him to reconnect with his family of origin. He joined a group hoping to do his reconstruction, but he simply could not do the prerequisite homework. One piece of that work is to draw up a chronology of facts in his life history. Listing in chronological order all the events of significance to him in his family would take him back into reliving his past. He simply could not do it. His childhood was too painful.

He did not believe he was strong enough to face the pain of that childhood, even though he was now thirty-three years old. He placed little faith in his adult resources that would enable him to handle the pain differently from the way he did as a child.

I lost contact with Ned, but I suspect that down the line he did do his reconnecting with his roots. He showed strength and wisdom in wanting to come to the group to begin with. He simply was not ready. The fear of pain kept him from doing what he knew someday he had to do. The fear of reliving pain keeps many from reconnecting with their roots.

Yet some of the most dramatic leaps forward in feeling confident, wholesome, strong, and good about the self that I have witnessed come when people are able to overcome their fears and reconstruct their families to see and understand the deep insecurities in their parents. They see how their parents were raised and how their parents' needs as children were not met; they see how their parents entered adulthood vulnerable and fragile. They are able to see their parents in the same human condition they find themselves, except that now those able to reconstruct and embrace their roots see that they indeed have progressed further than their parents ever did! Hope for the future and for their own children arises.

In contrast to those who have experienced much pain with their parents, we find those who think their parents come straight from heaven. And, surprisingly, this is the fourth powerful roadblock to completing the circle. These people have a very simple, childlike love and adoration of their parents. The thought of rebonding with them as coequals scares them too. They are afraid to get a more realistic picture of their parents. That would shatter the idealized perception they have. Such people, when asked, literally cannot think of any weakness or limits belonging to their parents. Many will idealize just one of the parents when the other parent is weak or absent.

Such people want to maintain this dreamy perception of their parents. Unfortunately, a certain romantic dependency results from this idealization of a parent. These childish pictures inhibit these people from being adults. They depend on their hero parent to sustain them. Thus, they reject changing their view of their parents. They will not see them in a new adult way. Their self-worth suffers because they reject themselves as adults and remain as children. Many of these people are doomed to live with low self-esteem because they will never be able to be as good as they think their parents are.

Having seen the reasons why people are reluctant to go home again, you may wonder, does anyone do it? Fortunately the journey of rerooting is undertaken by many. The result of their journey is to gain a greater sense of who they are, to feel the relief and joy in being compassionate with their parents, to experience a strength and inner resourcefulness that they never had before.

Chapter Six

Our Culture Says,
"Don't Do It"

❦

THE TV SERIES "ROOTS" still holds the record for the largest
viewing audience ever to watch a TV series. What explains this
phenomenon? It certainly was an interesting story, but TV has
given us many interesting stories. Strangely, it was about a black
American family. Most American theater offers us white subjects
for viewing.

Was it then some sort of white expiation ritual for the sins of
prejudice? If it had been a story focusing on the sinfulness of an
unjust social system, perhaps as a story on the Holocaust might
be, then that might be the reason for its popularity. We could say
watching "Roots" was a national purging process. But the focus of
"Roots" was much wider than the single topic of racial prejudice.

I believe "Roots" was popular because it struck at a missing
link in our American psyche, namely, the need to be connected
to our family roots. There is a way in which we Americans are
disassociated from our background and heritage. We tend to be
ahistorical, and this TV program spoke to that part of us that says
that our history is a vital part of us. We cannot do away with our
roots. Much of who and what we are comes from our lineage. The
TV series "Roots" was celebrating and honoring that part of us.
It said to us that our past family experience is important to us.

It is understandable why we tend to discount our history and

32

background. The European settlers, at least those after the original colonists, and later the Hispanics, struggled to be assimilated into the American melting pot. To this end, many parents refrained from speaking their native languages in front of their children. The effort to become American meant de-emphasizing one's foreign customs, traditions, and culture. A new culture and set of customs were being developed.

In the effort to become American old family ties, stories, and traditions were ignored or forgotten — or, at least, not handed down to the children. Cutting off one's past helped one to be in the melting pot. The task was to become a new kind of person, an American.

Along with the drive to de-emphasize the old family cultures and ties was the emphasis on the future. The frontier man became an American myth. To be American was to forget the past and push into new lands, new discoveries, new experiences. If you didn't like New York, you could go to Indiana. If Indiana didn't work, you joined the land rush to Oklahoma. And then there was the great pot of gold in California. The old was left behind. Is it any wonder that it is so easy for urban renewal to destroy old buildings to make room for the new? Thank God the Acropolis in Athens is not subject to urban renewal!

So today's American citizen often knows little of father's family and mother's family, and far less of the great grandparents.

There is another American myth that mitigates against putting any importance on one's family roots. It is the myth of the "self-made man," so well symbolized by John Wayne. The self-made man — that says it all. Man comes from nowhere and no one. He makes himself from scratch. No sissy dependence on roots, family of origin, lineage, and heritage. The true red-blooded American can do it all by himself. The solitary figure is standing on the open plain, in the sunset, killing off any enemy or opponent. The true American hero. The idol of the movie screen. This, the authentic American success story. To lean on one's roots goes against the grain of being independent — the John Wayne "Declaration of Independence."

Naturally, this effort to be self-made suggests the unimportance of being connected to an origin, a family of origin. The sooner one disconnects from depending on any family, the sooner one supposedly becomes self-made. The American myth downgrades connection to roots. There is seemingly no need of these roots once one is out of diapers.

There is good reason why the effort to become part of the American melting pot, to be a frontiersman, and to be a self-made man is so strong and well accepted in our culture. There is a certain validity to each of these three thrusts.

The value of the melting pot consisted of getting people of different ethnic, religious, and national backgrounds to function together in this new country. The effort was made to create a new person, the American, in place of the German, Irish, Italian, Polish, Spanish, Hungarian, Jewish, Catholic, Protestant, black, red, yellow, and white. Melt all these ingredients into a pot and create a new product: the American.

The value of the frontiersman was to be rid of the crippling aspects of the old, to forge new ways of doing, to create different responses to human needs.

The value of the self-made man was to take full responsibility for oneself, to be independent.

While there is a certain value in each of these three myths, we can also see their limitations. What has been debilitating to the individual person is the way the past, family roots, and tradition have been ignored, or even debased. If the effort to melt, embrace the new, and be self-sufficient could have been done while respecting, honoring, and using one's roots, then I do not think "Roots" would have been so relevant to our needs. It was precisely, in my opinion, because the American personality was starving for some bonding to family roots that the TV series was so popular. Because we had dishonored our roots, we needed to recapture them. "Roots" allowed us to get in touch with that missing piece of us. It gave permission for us to be connected to our lineage. This is Alex Haley's gift to us.

It gave us permission to do that because the TV series depicted how the offspring became strengthened and ennobled by honoring and being connected to their heritage and family of origin. The story of the family from generation to generation carried with it a pride, a strength, an honor that embraced each succeeding generation. It was as if each individual person walked through life facing enormous challenges, but not alone. Each person was more than just an individual. The power of the past lived on in each individual. It was an accumulation of energy that was passed on from generation to generation. Being rooted, connected to one's roots, only strengthened the persons rising from those roots. The story of one's forebears carried one along, sustaining each one's effort to forge a life for oneself. Carrying within one's soul the remembrances of one's roots gave one the energy and permission to develop one's own unique branch of the family tree.

To cut oneself off from one's roots, to ignore and turn one's back on those roots, would have diminished the Kunta Kintes of the world. That would have weakened the individuals coming along after them.

All this was sensed by the American public watching "Roots." A missing strain in our psyche was awakened. Perhaps as the members of that family advanced in human growth and dignity by being appropriately connected to their roots, so could we grow in strength and dignity.

There are signs of an American awakening to the need to honor our past and gain from it. Historical buildings are being preserved. Older neighborhoods are being restored, not destroyed. We are more conscious than ever of preserving our life, our past. We preserve forests, fauna, life species. More people are willing to preserve seashores and sea life. People are saving records and memorabilia for those following them. There are even computer software programs for making genograms!

We are at last beginning to realize that we can be strengthened by our past rather than be stuck in it. There is a growing interest in checking out where we came from, in understanding our parents' early experiences, in knowing what kind of people our great grandparents were.

Chapter Seven

Two Ingredients
Necessary for Self-Esteem

❧

I HAVE REFERRED TO SELF-ESTEEM in the previous pages. Today's literature on self-esteem speaks of many ingredients that make up the recipe for high self-worth. I want to comment on two because I have found them to be critical in enhancing people's self-esteem.

The first ingredient revolves around the reality of just who we are. In a sense we can say that we are made up of two basic parts. One part of us is our mother and father; the other part is our unique self. The following diagrams will help explain this reality.

Figure A represents the genetic package that we receive from our mothers and fathers. Figure B represents the relating and modeling of our fathers and mothers. From that experience with them we learn their meanings about life and events; we learn

Figure A

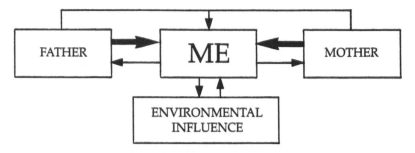

Lines represent forces of influence. Note—ME has a line of influence
also to MOTHER and FATHER, and to ENVIRONMENTAL INFLUENCE

Figure B

their values; we learn their ways of handling the experiences of daily life. From their modeling we learn their meaning of love, religion, trust, commitment, death, family, celebrations. From their relating we learn their meaning of what it is to be a man, woman, wife, husband, father, mother.

These two diagrams show how much we are part of our fathers and mothers. They are in us by way of genetics and influence.

However, we are not clones. We are unique, and our uniqueness is the other basic part of us. Our uniqueness stems from the way the twenty-three chromosomes from each parent combine in us, as exemplified by our fingerprints. In addition, our uniqueness stems from the way each of us reacts with our genetic equipment to the myriad influences of each day in our life. All these reactions help shape the unique way of thinking, feeling, and being that comprises our personality. Even identical twins have different fingerprints and personalities, even though there are striking similarities between them.

So one part of us contains our mother and father. The other part of us is that which resulted from the chromosomes combining and from the way we have reacted to life's experiences. This is the unique part of us.

Our reality, made up of these two basic parts, carries with it tremendous significance in regards to self-esteem.

High self-worth emanates from our being able to affirm and accept

ourselves as we are. Low self-worth results from disowning, con-
demning, and rejecting ourselves as we are. For example, if we
are negatively criticized by another and we internalize that criti-
cism, believe it to be true, then we feel negative about ourselves.
We reject ourselves in some way, which makes us feel bad about
ourselves.

If we fail to accept either or both of the two basic parts of
ourselves, then we have serious problems with our self-worth.
That is, if we do not affirm and accept the mother and father in
us, or if we not affirm and accept the unique part of ourselves,
then we will have poor self-worth.

Therefore, when we cannot understand and accept the humanity of the persons who are our mother and father, then we do
not accept that part of us which they are. The following diagram
(Figure C) further explains this.

Let us say that my father was abusive to me when I grew up
and as result I feared him. To cope with this fear I avoided him
and put him out of my mind. So today as an adult I have almost
completely blanked him out of my consciousness. Even though I
am trying to block out his abusiveness, the end result is that I blank
out all of him. Since he is a major part of me I am disregarding a
large piece of me, as the diagram below shows.

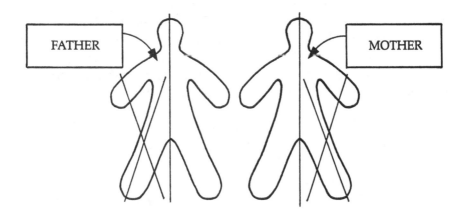

Figure C

By the same token, if I experienced my mother as weak and ineffectual, I can grow to despise her. In despising my mother, I am despising a part of me.

Because of what we have received from mother and father, both genetically and environmentally, whether we like it or not, they are part of us. We cannot destroy our chromosomes, nor can we destroy the influence they have had on us consciously and unconsciously. However, we can transform that influence, especially that which does not fit for us, just as the combining of each parent's twenty-three chromosomes was a biological transformation.

It is precisely because of this reality that returning to one's roots to accept them as part of us *is so crucial to our development and completion.* Our self-worth depends in large measure upon that acceptance.

Just as accepting our roots is important to our self-esteem, so accepting our uniqueness is equally important. This is why those people who fail to find themselves, be themselves, and express their unique selves are afflicted with low self-worth.

What I am saying here may raise a question. "What if there is a person in one's lineage who is evil or monstrous?" "What if I see my father or mother as abusive, hateful?" If such a person is part of one's roots, then how can that person be accepted?

While a person is performing a monstrous act, the person's action is to be rejected and stopped. No one should be permitted to inflict injustice upon another. However, there is a difference between the person acting in a moment in time and that person, him or herself. The despicable action does not define the person. If a man robs a bank, he is not essentially defined as a robber. He is a robber in that specific action.

In summary, the answer to enhancing my self-esteem is not to deny or eliminate the wicked persons in my roots but to accept them as human beings first and foremost, while not accepting them when they are acting destructively. Beneath and behind the monstrous behavior there is essentially a human struggling to survive with the genetic and environmental inheritance that is his or hers. Every baby coming from the womb has the same human desires that we all have, namely, to be loved, cared for, hugged, honored, understood, to survive, to feel good about oneself, to feel important, to be creative and expressive, to love, to enjoy. It is the human I can accept as symbolized by the personal name, not the monster symbolized by descriptive nouns like alcoholic, thief, abuser, killer, criminal.

The second ingredient crucial to self-esteem is to feel appropriately what one is. For example, if I am forty years old but feel and act like a teenager, then I am not feeling what I am, an adult. If I am a creative piano player but feel that I am a beginner, then I am not feeling what I am. If I am good-looking, yet feel that I'm not, then my perception does not square with my reality. If I am personable and generous, yet think that I am not very charitable and giving to others, there is a serious gap between my self-image and my reality. This inability to accept one's true reality is another way to reject oneself.

One of the most powerful ways to reject our true reality, and hence ourselves, is not to realize and accept that we are grown adults when in the presence of our parents.

I'll never forget one day when I was standing in my mother's living room talking to her. She was standing opposite me. In the midst of our conversation, I suddenly realized, "I'm taller than she is." I remembered feeling stunned. I was forty-three years old, 5'10"; she was eighty years old, 5'2." For all those years I had never realized that she was smaller than I!

If it took me so long to see that I was as tall, and indeed taller than she, how long did it take me to see that I was an equal to her, that she was as human as I? How long did it take me to *feel*, not like her child, but like a fully grown competent adult with as much authority as she had?

Achieving this realization with our parents takes time. It takes time to overcome the many years we lived in their presence as smaller than they, as less competent than they. It takes time to grow out of the impression that we need them for our well-being, that we are subservient to them. It takes time for us to realize that our self-worth does not depend upon their approval rather than upon our approval of ourselves.

Whatever time and effort it takes, it is critical to our self-worth that we accept ourselves as we really are. Vis-à-vis our parents, it means that we accept ourselves on a feeling level as the fully grown, coequal adults we are with them.

In summary, two vital ingredients to high self-esteem are to accept our parents and our roots as part of us and to accept ourselves as we are, fully grown and equal to our parents. Again, the way to do this is to perceive them as human rather than as parents. And the key to that is to go back to when our parents grew up, to see them born and raised as children.

Chapter Eight

Jim Ryan's Feeling of Unrest

&

THERE ARE SEVERAL WAYS we can go back to revisit the families our mother and father lived in, to see how they were raised. The following chapters will explain these several ways.

The first, and probably the most common, is that of conversing with our parents or their siblings. Since this approach is so important, I will illustrate it with the following story of Jim Ryan. While this story is fictional, it expresses a composite of my experience with people over many years.

Jim Ryan typifies many whom I have known in my professional years. At thirty-six, he reached a momentous decision in his life. He decided to embark on the journey of reconnecting with his parents. He wanted to understand them in a new and deeper way. Jim felt a need, at thirty-six, to see the persons behind the role of father, mother, stepmother — to perceive them as the full human beings they were. How did he come to this decision?

Jim's mother died when he was four. He gained a stepmother when he was seven, and their relationship was a successful one.

Several forces coalesced to bring Jim to his decision. For years he had secretly wondered about his mother, Bridget. There had been little conversation about her since her death, and especially after his father, Sean, had married Anna. At first Jim did not understand why all of a sudden not much was said about his mother. Later, he speculated that his father did not want to upset Anna in any way by referring to Bridget. At thirty-six, Jim decided that he would not be betraying his stepmother, Anna, by making inquiries into Bridget's life so that he could understand, appreciate, and accept her more completely as his biological mother.

As a growing child and teenager, Jim had unconsciously absorbed the message, from the silence about Bridget, that there was something wrong in trying to know his real mother. So over the years, Jim avoided considering that it might be important for him to know more about his mother. If his father had spoken openly about Bridget to Jim after her death and after marrying Anna, I suspect Jim would have taken steps much earlier to explore the life of his mother. Sean did leave the door open for Jim by seeing to it that Jim never lost contact with Bridget's sister, Eileen. As we will see later, Jim went to his Aunt Eileen to learn some early details about his mother.

There is something natural, deep inside each of us, that wants to be bonded closely with both of our biological parents. It was this natural instinct that finally surfaced and led Jim to decide to get to know his mother better. He felt estranged, not only by his lack of knowledge, but by his interpretation of Sean's silence that there was something wrong in knowing about her. It was like there was a gaping hole in Jim's life and something was missing. He felt incomplete.

Besides missing his mother, Jim began to feel a certain dissatisfaction with his life. He was successfully married with a wife and two children, had graduated from college, and was a successful manager in the corporate headquarters of one of the largest department stores in the United States. Jim could not put his finger on the cause of his growing unrest. Was he bored at work? Not necessarily. Was there something wrong at home? Again, nothing of major consequence seemed to be present.

One day when Jim and I were having lunch, Jim discussed this growing feeling of malaise. I tried to help him identify the precise source of his unrest, but we came up empty-handed. I asked him about his family background. It was then that he told me about Sean, Bridget, Anna, and Aunt Eileen.

I suggested that one way he might resolve his unrest was to start his journey back home again. Contrary to my experience with Howard and Susie, I was able, rather easily, to show Jim the value of knowing the members of his family of origin in a deeper way, as the full humans they were, not just as mother, father, aunt, uncle, grandfather, grandmother. Jim grew excited about the idea. He understood that his roots were part of him and to know himself better it was necessary to know his roots. I suspect Jim was easy to encourage because he had gone so long with an empty feeling about his mother.

I also explained a very important lesson I had learned over the years in helping individuals and married couples with their problems. I told him that I have come to appreciate more acutely how we tie up vast amounts of energies with issues emanating from our family of origin that should have been resolved years ago. Tying up such energies deprives us of using them for the problems facing us in our current life. The most frequent piece of unfinished business is that of being *improperly* connected to our root system.

Jim was not aware of just how much of his energy was consumed in inappropriately connecting to his family roots, and, specifically in his case, in coping with the emptiness of not having much connection to such an important root as his mother. I told him, "You concluded that it was not right to learn about Bridget, especially after your dad married Anna. You have diverted much energy over the years in restraining yourself from pursuing a very natural quest and in dealing with the hidden sadness and emptiness that produces."

Jim was fascinated with this concept. He asked for another example. "All right," I said, "a less dramatic but very common inappropriate connecting is when at thirty-two, forty-five, or sixty, we still relate to our parents more as parents than as humans equal to us. That is, we find ourselves behaving at home with our parents in much the same way as we did when were teenagers or even younger. We are not as free in their presence as we are with our friends or spouses. The reason for this is that we perceive ourselves as children and them as parents. We are relating to them in a child-to-parent relationship rather than in an adult-to-adult or person-to-person relationship. In other words, Jim, if we really had an emotional, gut feeling for them as human beings just as we experience ourselves, then many of our fears, inhibitions, and inappropriate defenses would disappear."

"How's that?," Jim asked.

"We would not be so anxious to get their approval," I said.

"Well, we don't want to hurt them" Jim said. "I mean, if I were to treat my father as equal to me rather than as my father, I might hurt him."

"Of course we don't want to hurt them," I said. "We don't want to hurt anyone, especially those close to us. This is not a matter of hurting our parents; it is a matter of seeing them as they really are. For example, have you ever imagined what went on when Bridget and Sean first laid eyes on each other?"

"No," said Jim.

"Have you ever imagined how they dated?" I continued.

"No, not really. Oh, I know a few things they did. They went dancing for instance. But I haven't tried to inquire or imagine how they dated and felt about each other," Jim said.

"That's right," I answered. "Most of us don't." Superficially we may know there were some romantic feelings, some strong pulls, perhaps even some jealousies, but we have never given much attention to that. And to the degree that we haven't emotionally connected to that, we have not incorporated Sean and Bridget inside of us as the complex, vulnerable, sexual, idealistic, youthful, shy, awkward persons they were.

"Do you know what it was like for your father to grow up in his family? Do you know if he felt put down, inferior at times? Do you know what worried him, scared him as a seven-year-old, eleven-year-old, sixteen-year-old? Do you know what meanings he made of life as he watched his parents in action?"

"Not really," said Jim. "I've never asked him those questions point blank. He has referred to some of his early childhood experiences; I know his folks, my grandparents. I guess I have inferred some of the answers to your questions, but by and large they are educated guesses on my part. It would be interesting to know the answers to those questions."

I sat silently as Jim was thinking about these issues. Then he blinked his eyes and came back to me; he smiled as if he had taken a small step in fantasizing the young Sean and Bridget — seeing them as simple human beings, not as godlike parents. He picked up the conversation again. "Yes, I would like to know how it was for my mom and dad before they married. But what was that point you were making about our energies being tied up. You say it keeps our resources tied up. I don't quite know what you are driving at."

"I understand your confusion," I said. "It has been amazing to me to realize how much energy we do siphon off from our daily concerns to tend to the unfinished business with our family of origin. When I began counseling and doing family therapy, I knew theoretically that energy is tied up in issues of the past. But I had no idea how *much* energy is expended with the old and how seriously that can keep us from meeting the challenges of daily events. I think that many of us operate on half energy."

I then drew Jim this diagram on one of the paper napkins.

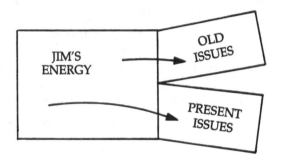

Figure D

"You see, Jim, if a large portion of your energy is consumed in dealing with the emptiness and sadness about your mother, then you don't have your full resources to deal with your current life. Could your unrest be simply due to that? That is, if you are distracted from the call of your present life, your wife, kids, job, leisure, spiritual life by tending to the past, how fully satisfied could you be? Remember the times you were fully focused, turned on, fully present. It may have been that unforgettable act of love, that extraordinary tennis match, that glorious vacation, solving a major crisis at work. You felt fully alive didn't you?"

"Yes, I did," replied Jim.

"That was because at those moments, in those events, you were able to muster together all of your energy and resources," I said. "After those times, half your energy, or some part of it, unconsciously drifted back to the unsettled issues of your root system.

"Jim, I want to tell you something. I've just written an article dealing with this — and indeed challenging some old ways of thinking about family therapy. I want to give it to you. One of my points in this article is that perhaps, when it is all said and done, we therapists ought not to deal with people's problems as presented to us. For example, with you, perhaps we should not try to figure out what you are restless about — job, marriage, growing old, whatever. But rather, the effort should be to help you get *appropriately* connected to *your* roots, which will free up your energy and make it available to you in your life today. With all of your energies in focus you will be able to solve the problem of restlessness yourself. In other words, Jim, only *you* know what's best for you, only *you* have the internal resources to figure it out and go in the right direction."

"But how do you know this, Bill?" Jim asked.

"It is a conviction that comes out of my years of experience, especially in doing family reconstruction, i.e., helping people have these new, human, appropriate connections to parents, grandparents, aunts, and uncles. I have seen so many wonderful results happen to people in their lives. Not only do they make peace with their roots, but many solidify their marriages; others gain health, smile more; some get out of toxic situations at work or in relationships; many change careers; others relate better with their children."

We ended our conversation and I promised I would send the article.

Chapter Nine

Jim Prepares
to Go Home Again

❧

JIM CALLED ME a week after our conversation. He was excited. He had read the article. He wanted to know if I had any ideas to help him with reconnecting to his family of origin. We had another lunch together.

I told Jim of my own experiences in taking this journey and of my experiences helping others do it. "I'll never forget, years ago I was traveling with my mother from San Jose to San Diego. I was alone in the car for ten hours with her. I began to ask her all sorts of questions about her childhood, why she got married to her first husband and then to my father. I asked her questions about my dad, who had died twelve years earlier, and about their relationship. She talked on and on. I learned things I'd never known before. She was very honest. She bared her soul. It was such a wonderful experience. I appreciated, as I had never done before, just how human she was, how vulnerable. I felt so close to her and honored that she trusted me enough to tell me all those things about herself. I think she was honored by my inquiry into her life. She said that some of these things she had never told anyone. I sensed a relief in her. She was getting some things off her chest, some burdens she carried all alone. Now she was sharing that with someone. She was not alone.

"I'll never forgot her honesty, her trusting me, and the things she said about her childhood, her relationship to her parents, and her relationship with my dad. Later on, when things got sticky between us, I'd remember what she said and I could see her as the vulnerable human she was. It softened me toward her; that was important because my mother was so competent, strong, energetic most of the time. It also helped me be more compassionate with her whenever she would don her righteousness. I could now see more clearly that her need to be right or to have it done her way was how she learned to cope with the many uncertainties and insecurities of her past life. Before that ten-hour trip I had no knowledge of this side of my mother.

"I could also tell her some things about myself that up to that moment I was afraid to tell her. As the hours went on the trust grew. She was not critical of me as I explained some of my life to her, some of my vulnerabilities. We were just two adult humans, special friends, sharing our inner lives with each other in open honesty.

"I often wished I had had a similar conversation with my dad before he died. And so I miss him more these days than I do my mother, although my mother died in 1981 and my father in 1960. I seem complete with her, but not as complete with my father. However, what my mother told me and doing my family reconstruction added much to what I knew about him. I feel closer to him after my conversations with Corinne, my mother, and after doing my family reconstruction."

Jim was listening intently. "I hope I have that same experience with my father, but I'm afraid," Jim said.

"I know, most people who take this step are afraid. They want the best from their parents. They hope for much honesty and welcome openness. But never having had this kind of conversation, naturally it scares them. You'd hate to be turned down. Jim, I can assure you from my experience with those who have tried to learn these things from their past, 90 percent have been successful. Only a few are turned away by a parent.

"Jim, if you are rebuffed, know this for a certainty: It is only because your father is threatened by your inquiries. He is afraid, for some reason, to be open with you. Only God knows how he may be scared. Perhaps he'll feel disloyal to his parents if he tells you of some pain they caused him; perhaps he'll be afraid you'll think less of him; perhaps he'll be jittery because he may never have told anyone before what you are asking of him; perhaps he will be afraid to say anything negative about your mother; or he may feel that in being honest about Bridget he will be disloyal to Anna. Who knows what may scare him. But stay firm in knowing that if he does rebuff you, *it is not a rejection of you,* but due to some fear on his part. He may even fear hurting you!

"If your father welcomes your inquiries and you have a visit in which you can share back and forth, I think that you will find some lasting results occur. You'll find yourself able to accept your father more, and be able to drop your need to change him, your need to get him to be more approving and accepting of you. You will both have a deeper compassion for the dreams and struggles, sorrows and joys that have been part and parcel of both of your lives."

Jim thanked me for this encouragement and warning.

About a month later I got another phone call from Jim. He had just returned from Hutchison, Kansas, where his dad and Anna live. He was ecstatic. He had taken his father to Kansas City to see the Kansas City Royals play the Boston Red Sox in a night ball game. They had spent the night in Kansas City and had returned to Hutchinson the next day. Jim said, "Bill, I had a most wonderful time visiting with my dad. We spent the entire afternoon and next morning together. He told me things I had never known before. I thought of you and your mother traveling from San Jose to San Diego. When can we meet? I want to tell you all about it."

In order to help the reader through this story of Jim, I include the genograms of his three families on the next page. Note that I have added Jim's marriage to Kathy with their two children.

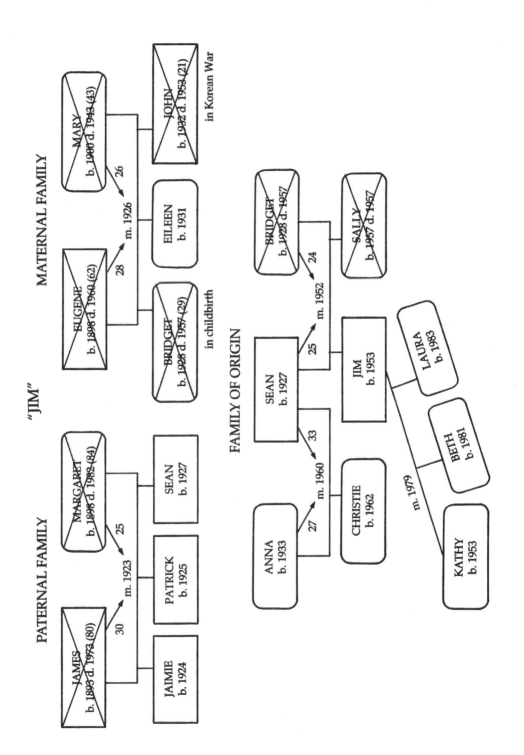

"JIM"

PATERNAL FAMILY

MATERNAL FAMILY

FAMILY OF ORIGIN

Chapter Ten

Jim's Trip—A Success

ᔐ

JIM BROUGHT HIS WIFE, KATHY, to lunch with me at my suggestion. I wanted Kathy to share in the experience. Often in telling the story to a third person other details, resources, and feelings may emerge. Learning more about Jim's father, Sean, would allow Kathy to know Jim better, for *Sean is part of Jim.* Also, Jim was now a changed person, for this conversation with Sean had altered Jim's perceptions of his father. This new perception changed the way Jim thought and felt about himself on some deep level. Therefore, it was important for Kathy to understand the genesis of this change in Jim.

Jim had brought a tape recorder with him on the trip. He had asked his dad's permission to tape much of the conversation so that perhaps later on, when Jim's kids were older, they could hear the story from Sean and feel closer to their roots. Sean had agreed on the condition that if he said anything that he did not want anyone else to know, it would be erased.

Jim began. "It was a little awkward at first. I was nervous and Dad, I think, sensed that." He then turned on the recorder. The following are excerpted from the tape.

"Dad, I've been thinking lately about my life. I guess I have more time now that the family is well on its way and I seem to know all the ins and outs of my job. As you know, Kathy is the best. She is a wonderful mother to the kids. My life is blessed compared to many I work with.

"But, you know what? Recently most of my thinking has been about my background rather than about my future. There is a way I have grown more curious about you, Anna, and, of course, Mother. I have even forgotten some things about my early years. Well, the fact is, Dad, I'd really like to know you better. Even though I knew Grandmother and Grandfather [they are dead now], there is still so much I don't know. Do you mind if we spend some time with this?"

SEAN: "Well, I don't know. I always assumed you knew all there was to know. I mean, you knew all that was important to know. We visited your grandparents enough to know them. That's what's important. But if it helps any, I'll give it a shot. What do you want to know?"

JIM: "Well, for starters, do you know anything more about your birth other than it was in 1927 in Boston?"

SEAN: "I know that my parents went to Mass more frequently during the weeks preceding my birth, praying for a safe delivery. They considered the three of us kids as gifts from God — you know how religious both of them were. I was born in St. Mallory's Hospital about four in the morning, Mother told me. Dad was there. It was a normal birth, I guess. At least, I've never heard any differently."

JIM: "I know they named you after Margaret's favorite brother, Sean. Is there anything else about your name?"

SEAN: "Well, no. I've always liked my name. Uncle Sean was a great guy. He lived down the street from us when I was growing up, and I think I was his favorite. He took me to the Red Sox games a couple of times a year. That was special. Dad was more into reading and labor activities. Uncle Sean was a little looser than Dad. I mean, he didn't seem to take life so seriously as Dad. Dad was always fighting for some cause. Sean was more for dancing the jig! In Dad and Sean I had good models, wouldn't you say? Incidentally, Dad always enjoyed Sean visiting us. He brought laughter to us all. No wonder mother liked him so much. They say he used to be quite a ladies man, but I don't know much about that."

JIM: "What was it like for you growing up in your home?"

SEAN: "I guess we were pretty normal. We knew our place and what was expected of us. Mother and Dad were good religious people, you know. The church meant a lot to them. I went to public

school, but everyone there seemed to be either Irish Catholic or
Italian Catholic. I think most of the teachers were Catholic. We
stayed pretty much in the neighborhood, and much of our social
activity was at the church. Of course the Depression hit about
1930. Things were a little rough for a while but luckily Dad kept
his job as a printer for the *Boston Globe*. We were able to help
other members of Dad's and Mother's families who lost their jobs.
We all cut back in those days and shared our food and clothes.
There was never a question about taking someone in or helping
someone. Uncle Sean was good about that too."

JIM: "What about you? What made you feel good and what
brought pain? Surely you had some rough spots — we all do."

SEAN: "I always felt taken care of. I felt loved by my family. I
was blessed with good parents."

Pause.

JIM: "But what were some of your problems?"

SEAN: "When I was in the fifth grade I got sick with some
strange sickness. I don't think they ever figured out what it was.
Maybe it was some sort of flu or some bug or something. But I got
sicker than a dog, vomiting, fever, weak. Later they told me they
thought I'd die. I never knew that at the time. It was a surprise to
me to know that I was that sick. I was out of school for some time,
and when I went back I was far behind, especially in arithmetic. It
seems I never caught up, especially in math. The teacher was on
my back; Mother was worried. Dad was funny. He didn't seem
to care much about math — literature was important to him. I
remember one night hearing Mother and Dad argue about this.
Mother wanted Dad to get after me, feeling she was the only one
concerned. Dad was saying he was suspicious of people clever
with figures and that it was more important to understand the
thoughts of mankind than the figures of bankers. Incidentally,
did I ever tell you that Dad would sit us all down each evening
and read poetry to us? He read it so we could understand it too!"

JIM: "How did all that affect you?"

SEAN: "The poetry reading?" (with a grin in his voice)

JIM: "No, you know what I mean."

SEAN: "Well, I never did get good in math. Oh, I passed okay,
but I guess I took after Dad. But I think it got me down. I mean, the
conflict between Mother and Dad about my poor grades in math
and later in chemistry and physics. I don't know why Mother was

such a stickler about math. Jaimie and Patrick [Sean's brothers] were whizzes in math. Well, you know that; Pat at MIT in science and Jaimie a major partner in Arthur Anderson.

"I felt I was causing a problem between Mother and Dad. God, I never thought of this till now! When I was four years old I accidentally let our dog out the kitchen door, and that afternoon he was killed by a car. When Dad returned home all hell broke out. Gosh, I have forgotten that till now. That was terrible! Dad blamed Mother for not watching me more carefully. Dad loved that dog; he was named King Lear after Shakespeare's King Lear. You know, now, as I think about it, I never heard my parents so angry with each other. I thought I had committed a major crime. It's funny.

"You know when you go to confession you tell the priest your sins. Well, sometimes in the early grades I couldn't think of a sin so I told the priest about the sin of letting King Lear out the door. I remember the priest laughed behind that dark screen. Funny the things we do as kids —

"I guess from that time on I was very careful not to cause any conflict between my parents. So I felt very bad about the math deal. The harder I tried to make up the math grade, the worse it got. Would there be more fights over this, I worried? I felt bad too, that I wasn't as good as Jaimie and Pat.

"I don't think I ever got over that inferior feeling till in high school when I became a star athlete and got the lead parts in the school plays."

(A long silence)

JIM: "I never knew about that, Dad. Thanks for telling me that."

(A long pause)

SEAN: "You know, Jim, you never caused any trouble between your mother and me. We were so happy with you. Your mother was a wonderful person, Jim."

JIM: "Tell me about her. My memories are so vague."

SEAN: "Yes, I guess they are. I guess I haven't told you as much about her as I should have. I didn't want to upset Anna, you know. I mean, I don't think it would have, but I didn't want to risk it in our early years in the marriage. I didn't want you to think you were the cause of any conflict between us.

"Your mother was a lot like my Uncle Sean. She was fun-loving, laughed a lot, teased me into taking risks. She lightened my life. I still miss her."

(Silence... a tear)

"Damn! why did she die like that! It's been very hard to accept her death, Jim. I've never told you this. I tried to comfort you as best I could. I told you it was the will of God. I tried to be courageous with you so you could take it. But down deep — I don't know — I still can't figure it out. I guess what helps, Jim, is that you've turned out so well. I was crushed but had to act strong. I think my innards were in shock, numb, and my outers functional."

(Turning to Jim) "I think I'm angry, Jim. Right now, I think I'm angry. Yes, I am. I am angry, and it's not right to be. Oh, God. This is dumb. Why are you asking me all this, Jim?"

(A long, long silence; a calming down)

"Thanks, Jim. I needed that. Whew, I didn't know that was all inside me. I feel better now. She was a great gal."

"How do you feel?"

JIM (with tears): "Thanks, Dad. I feel real close to Mother right now, like I'm there, right with you and her. I've been crying too as you've talked and been silent. I feel I want to know so much more about her. Can you tell me more?"

SEAN: "Sure. I'd be happy to. I'll tell you all you want to know..."

From here on Sean shared many stories and feelings about Bridget, their early dating, proposal to marry, their marriage, honeymoon, the four years of their marriage, their joy in the pregnancy; the ecstasy of Jim's birth, the hopes for the future; and another pregnancy, and the death of Bridget and Sally in childbirth.

By the time they got to the baseball game, Jim and Sean had completed the grieving process that had remained unfinished for both of them for all those years. They watched the game in a trance, a drained sort of way, detached from who won or lost. The game allowed the energy to shift and let them go in and out of their thoughts whenever they wanted to.

That night in Kansas City, they had a restful sleep, and both slept late the next morning.

Chapter Eleven

Jim's Journey Changes Him

❧

THE NEXT MORNING on the way back to Hutchinson, Sean said, "We got sidetracked yesterday afternoon from my upbringing, didn't we? We spent most of the time talking about your mother. Is there anything more you'd like to know, Jim?" It was as if Sean was hoping Jim would ask more about his own family.

Jim replied, "Yes, there is more. There is a lot more I'd like to know. Let me think.... How do you think your dad related to you and you to him?" Jim asked.

SEAN: "I think he was a little more relaxed with me than with Jaimie and Pat. He admired my interest in literature; I guess I took after him in that way. I think in some way he wanted me to do more than he did. He printed the word; I think he wanted me to write the word. But he tried to be accepting of all of us. I looked up to Dad, admired him. He gave me a zest for the cause of justice — not just personal morality but a social morality. He got that somehow from the church maybe; I don't know.

JIM: "That sounds almost too good to be true. What were some of the negatives?"

SEAN: "I'm a little confused about this. I guess I don't know what he did with his anger, irritations, disappointments, sadness. Did he have any? Did he pray them away? I don't know."

JIM: "Well, he was angry with Margaret about the dog."

SEAN: "That's right. He blamed Mother for that. He was angry! But that was the only time I remember; and I had forgotten

57

that till yesterday. There were other irritations. He'd get after us boys, but even then he'd do it in a way that made sense. I mean, we knew we were wrong. All he had to do is look at us and we felt bad. And, by and large, the three of us were good boys."

JIM: "Well what about you and your mother."

SEAN: "Again I saw her as a person who would always be there for us. She was understanding. She was more fun-loving than Dad in one way, and stricter in another. She was really a bug about excelling in school. That was something I didn't understand. Yet, she was the one who pushed for the parties, singing, and going to church dances. She loved to tell jokes. I swear I never knew where she picked them up. So she was a little looser with us than Dad, and we felt a little freer with her. I felt more affection and tenderness for her, and looked up more to Dad. I feel maybe I was a disappointment to her in later years, as I haven't become as prestigious as Jaimie and Pat."

(Sean was a sales rep of a large publishing house in New York City.)

JIM: "Well, how did James and Margaret relate to each other?"

SEAN: "They had a lot of respect for each other and were tender to each other, especially Dad toward Mother. I'd say she was more on the side of respecting him, and he was more on the side of being affectionate with her — although they both loved and respected each other. Once in a while they would disagree about us, but not much. As I said, we didn't give them too much trouble. One of the things that did bother me about their relationship is the way Mother, I think, would dig at Dad about his job. He would be made offers by the paper to go higher, get into management, but he'd always refuse, saying he couldn't turn his back on the workers. He was a leader in the union movement, you know. I think Mother was confused. On the one hand she admired his sense of justice and fighting for the underdog. After all, we Irish were the underdogs for so long in this country. On the other hand she wanted him to advance in this world, and it bothered her to see Dad turn down chances to advance. Dad was plenty smart, and I think he would have made a super manager — even editor if he ever put his hand to writing. He read so much. He wrote wonderful stuff for the union newspaper. He was always in on the contract bargaining sessions."

Jim pursued other questions that morning with Sean. Jim

asked such things as what scared or threatened Sean's parents and how they coped? Did they fight at any other times? How did they deal with what irritated them about each other? How did they show their love to each other? Jim's curiosity seemed to have no limit. He asked Sean what made his father feel good about himself? What got his father down? Jim asked the same questions regarding Sean's mother. What limitations did you see in your mother and father; what strengths? What assets and liabilities do you think you got from each of them.

Jim asked Sean what he learned about what it means to be a man, a husband, a father? What makes him happy? What are his cherished values? What makes him feel guilty? What scares or threatens him the most and how does he deal with that?

He asked Sean what happened to him when he entered puberty. What kinds of girls were good-looking to him. Jim asked about Sean's first date. How did Sean learn about sex and how to conduct himself with women? What questions did he have that went unanswered? What embarrassed him? Jim then inquired, if Sean had to relive his life at home, was there anything he wished would have been different? How did he wish he would have been different, or his father and mother different toward him?

When Jim was through reliving his visit to his father, he turned to me and asked two questions. "Bill, there are two things that I don't understand about Dad. First, why didn't he do better financially and at work? I always think he felt frustrated in his job. While he liked selling and being with people, I think there was an artistic sense about him that he never developed. He blocked himself in some way. I think he would have been happier writing in some way — either as a novelist or on a newspaper.

And secondly, I still can't figure out why he never talked about Mother after her death. It was almost as if she never existed. In a way I felt like a motherless child. He talked freely about her in Kansas City. Why not earlier? I understand his fear of intimidating Anna, but there must be more to it than that."

I asked, "Jim, I want to see if you want to answer a personal question I have of you; and Kathy, would you mind if he answers? The question is this. Is there any way, Jim, that you feel you hold back from Kathy? I mean do you feel as open and giving to Kathy as she does to you? Kathy, do you mind the answer from Jim?"

Kathy said, "No."

"Jim, do you want to answer?"

Jim said, "Yes, you are right, Bill. How did you suspect? I think I'm more bothered by it than Kathy is. There is some mysterious way I feel constrained or inhibited. I don't know. The times I feel I am giving fully are rarer than the many times Kathy is so giving to me. I guess that is a third puzzle for me. Have any hunches, Bill?"

Chapter Twelve

Unraveling Jim's Three Mysteries

❧

"**Y**ES, I HAVE SOME CLUES," I replied. "Let's pursue them and see if the three of us can't figure out the answers to your questions. I'll tell you what I think might be going on, but you, Jim, are the only one who can ultimately judge what the answers might be. Sean and Bridget are part of you and in you. You know more than you think you know. Trust your intuition.

"In regard to your first question — why didn't your dad do more in life workwise? Now all I'm going to say to you about your dad is stuff that *may* have been going on in his *unconscious* mind more than consciously. That is, if you asked your dad, he may not know the answer to this question.

"I suspect Sean did have literary talents. He did read a lot and took after his dad in that way. He certainly didn't show any brilliance for math or science! Yet he ended up much like his dad, who could have gone higher, could have even been a writer, a reporter, an editor. Perhaps Sean didn't want to outstrip his dad. If Sean had become a writer rather than a seller of books, he might have felt disloyal to his father. He might have felt that his success was a further dig at his father, just as Margaret would subtly put him down for not taking the opportunities to go higher at the paper. He didn't want to hurt his dad any further.

"Also, perhaps Sean did not utilize his capacity as a way to rebel secretly against his mother, who kept nipping at him to excel in school 'like Jaimie and Patrick.' As you describe Sean's family, they weren't very open about what bugged them. Sean never said to his mother, 'Get off my back, lay off! I don't like math, I'd rather read. What's with you anyway? What's the push to excel in math?' This might have relieved Sean and allowed him to pursue his talents more openly. *Suppressing anger like that can tie up one's energies and resources.* It doesn't allow a person to see things more clearly.

"If that is the case," Jim asked, "why didn't Sean say this to his mother, show his anger?"

"Perhaps because James and Margaret were too good! Sean only saw his dad snap back, get angry at Margaret once. Sean seldom saw his parents angry, out of control, surly, 'bad.' His parents were godlike. So how do you expect Sean to confront a god! How could a kid even think differently than god! Since Jim and Margaret didn't argue much in front of the kids, the kids felt the parents were right in every way. There was no permission to disagree; there was no modeling of one god opposing the other god. And since they were such good parents, it was hard to see any human weaknesses that would allow Sean to see them as fully human. It was too threatening to be angry at god. It is easier to be angry at a fellow human. So Sean felt constrained from blowing off at Margaret. When a person can't be open about what's bugging him, then often such a person will express the anger indirectly. Perhaps Sean indirectly expressed his anger by rebelling in not becoming what Margaret wanted him to become. The lack of the direct expression of anger in the home also sets a norm for Sean: 'No anger is to be shown here.'

"So for fear of betraying his dad and as a way to express suppressed anger perhaps, Sean never pursued his natural interests in literature. Sean's resources were derailed in the effort to deal with the suppressed anger. What do you think, Jim?"

"Well, I'll have to think about that. At least nothing occurs to me that says it's wrong," said Jim. "What do you think, Kathy?"

Kathy responded, "Well, I never thought of it before, but now something begins to make sense. I've felt something was missing in your father. But I could never put my finger on it. In fact I've never had words for it, until now. I think that there was something too good about the Ryan family. They were too good to be true. Something of the real was missing. Yes, that's it. I never could identify what seemed a little strange about your family. But it fits now. Perhaps Bill is on to something — I don't know."

I repeated, "Just think about it, Jim. What's important is to realize that there are deeper reasons why a person doesn't seem to reach fulfillment. And whatever those reasons are, they make human sense. When you see that, then you will appreciate your father in a more human way. Your compassion grows and you make your dad more a part of you."

"Remember my first point. All this — or whatever it is — is more in Sean's unconsciousness than in his awareness."

Then Jim said, "All right, but explain Margaret's insistence that Sean excel in math and science when it was so clear that his natural aptitudes were like James's, that is, in literature?"

"Well," I replied "perhaps Margaret saw that very clearly and it scared her."

"What do you mean, Bill?" asked Jim. "How could that scare her?"

"Maybe Margaret, in seeing Sean so much like his father, feared her son might end up like him — unfulfilled, at least that's the way Margaret saw her husband," I answered. "So, being afraid that Sean would be unfulfilled like his father, she tried to turn him from his interest in letters (turn him from being like his father) and interest him in another field. Surely if Jaimie and Patrick were stars in math, why couldn't Sean excel there too?

"The evidence was beginning to mount at school that the two older boys were clipping along at full steam, truly fulfilling themselves, utilizing fully their natural talents — something their father hadn't done. Margaret sensed that Sean was more closely bonded to his father than the other two boys. This added to her fears perhaps. So on an unconscious level Margaret coped with her fears by trying to push Sean into a different field of endeavor, one in which the other two boys were doing well."

"Why was Margaret so scared about Sean not being fulfilled?" Jim asked. "I mean, I can understand the normal desire to have your children happy, fulfilled, but if you're right, Bill, it seems that Margaret was more than normally concerned with this issue."

"I think you're right, Jim," I replied. "It is hard to tell what it was that upset Margaret so much that she couldn't go along with Sean's natural proclivities and support his interest in literature. In other words, why did James's lack of advancement and her fear of

Sean following those footsteps disturb her deeply? Did Margaret as a child suffer in some way because her father was unhappy and unfulfilled? Was she just very ambitious and wanting to climb higher in the world? Was she embarrassed about being Irish and part of the working class? Whatever it was I'm sure that Margaret didn't know herself what was triggering this more than average concern about being fulfilled. I think you yourself said that Margaret did admire her husband for his labor organizing activities, his courage in that struggle, his concern for others. So Margaret was conflicted and perhaps could never see very clearly what was going on in her insides. As I say, I don't know. My speculation may trigger some thoughts of your own later on, Jim."

"Hummm, that's very interesting. I'll give some thought to that," Jim said. "What about my second question, why did Dad not speak to me of Bridget after she died and especially after he married Anna?"

"Well, Jim, two powerful things may have been going on in your dad that could explain his behavior," I answered. "It is obvious from your conversation with Sean that the death of Bridget and the baby was a most painful blow. It was painful on several levels. Just the event itself carries enough pain for any one human being. I think your father and mother were terrifically in love; that's just a hunch I have. [Jim's eyes begin to soften and tear up.] The sudden and unexpected death at the very height of her life, in the full flowering of her hopes and dreams and happiness, was such a shock to Sean that I think he couldn't let the full force of his pain and loss hit him. I think Sean survived, as I suspect most of us would have, by suppressing that pain or distracting himself from that pain. Sean's pain was not only overwhelming, but it was terrifying — if the pain was fully felt it might overwhelm him.

"Now this being so, Sean feared for you, Jim. He feared that pain might overwhelm you. On an unconscious level he might have felt that if you felt your pain, you also might not survive. So in order to protect you, not only for your sake, but for his sake too, he tried to keep the pain from you. And the way he did this was not to talk about Bridget. If he could get you to forget about her to some degree, then he would protect you from your pain. He helped you cope with the overwhelming loss the way he was coping — not to think about her. So perhaps as Sean survived by suppressing the pain, he felt that he could help you the same way."

I could see the light bulbs go on in Jim's mind, his face lightened up, his eyes widened, he leaned forward, his face was relaxed. "That makes sense, Bill," Jim exclaimed. A long pause. We sat there respecting what was going on inside Jim.

Jim turned to Kathy, taking her hand, tears again in his eyes. "That explains it, doesn't it?" Kathy smiled softly at Jim. "Yes, dear." I excused myself to leave them to themselves.

The next chapter reveals the solution to the third mystery concerning Jim's intimacy with Kathy.

Chapter Thirteen

The Aftermath

❧

ABOUT THREE DAYS LATER Jim called me. "Bill, I can't tell you what has come over me. I don't know all the reasons, but there is a way I feel so much closer to Kathy. These have been the most solid, intimate three days of our marriage. I feel an enormous weight off my shoulders, and I don't know why."

"How do you feel about your dad?" I asked.

"Very close, Bill," Jim answered. "Again I don't know what's happened. I think in some way, while I've loved and respected my dad, I've held a grudge against him for shutting Mother out of my life. But I've never been aware of that till now. And the grudge is gone! It's funny, Bill, how you have such a grudge all these years and do not even know it. I think there was some anger inside of me. But I feel cleansed inside now, like all that's passed. What's going on?"

"Well, Jim, your visit with your dad has occurred at a moment in your life when you were most ready for this. I mean it's like the splinter that was deeply imbedded in the finger and has been gradually moving up to the surface and is now sticking its head out to be plucked out by tweezers.

"You had the visit with your father; you had two very important questions buzzing around in your head and an answer to those questions that apparently made a great deal of sense to you. When that happened you were able to understand your dad emotionally, in a way you have never understood him before.

66

Understanding what was going on inside of him, behind that external behavior of silence about your mother, has given you the capacity to be compassionate with him. You feel his feelings, not just know his thoughts. That understanding, that compassion, has allowed you to accept him as he is. As a result you no longer carry that hidden grudge and anger toward him. You understand now why he kept his silence; you feel with him in his skin and feel the panic that drove him to his silence. You can appreciate him as the struggling human being he was, trying to save you and himself from the pain he feared might occur. You feel close to him now and the weight of that grudge and anger is gone.

"Add to that the emotional bonding you now have with your long lost mother, Bridget. Your visit with Sean has begun to fill you up with your mother. The energy tied up in dealing with a lost mother is now released.

"All the energy tied up in carrying the suppressed anger and the missing mother is now released so you can focus on your present life. So it allows you to be closer to Kathy, whom you love so much. At least this is part of what I see has happened and it explains what is going on with you."

"Perhaps you're right, Bill. Thanks again, and can I call you down the line?"

"Of course," I said. "I'm anxious to see what happens if and when you ask Aunt Eileen about your mother's early upbringing. But take your time. You have traveled a very long journey. You may need time to assimilate all your experiences. Goodbye, Jim."

Chapter Fourteen

The Essence of Change
Is in the Heart

❧

THE STORY OF JIM RYAN is one in which the relationship between Jim and his father changed due to the transactions that occurred between them. *The change of the relationship is not the point of this book.* The point is that the change occurs within the individual person who is reclaiming his or her roots in a new way. For many of us, a change in the actual relationships with parents and other members of one's family system is not possible. These people may be dead. Or the family members may resist any change in the ongoing relationship. What *is* important is that we perceive and feel our parents, our family roots, in a new way within our hearts. It is within our internal psychological makeup that we shift from perceiving simply parents to perceiving full human beings.

I emphasize this because often a person badly wants the actual relationship to change. This, of course, is understandable. However, if our thrust is to change the relationship, this could hinder the change within ourselves. The energy is not directed to the proper goal.

Ironically, when the energy is properly directed to changing our own internal perceptions of our parents, then often the relationship among living family members does change, whereas in the past it had not changed. This is because when a grown son or daughter, unconsciously or consciously, tries to force a change in the way parents relate to him or her, the parents feel threatened and resist such efforts. On the other hand, when a son or daughter is content with an internal change in perception of the parents, that person can drop the demand that the parents change. When this demand is dropped, the parents somehow recognize the change in their son or daughter, feel no threat, and can on their own change the way they relate to their son or daughter. If this change continues, the parents begin to sense that their child is a full person, coequal to them. The parents may sense that an adult-to-adult relationship is by far the better one to have both for themselves as well as for their grown children.

Buried in the story of Jim Ryan is a series of questions, inquiries, lines of probing that any one can use in gathering data that is very useful in changing one's perception of one's parents. Often this information can be gathered from other relatives or friends of one's parents. As you can see, these inquiries deal mainly with understanding a parent when that person was a child growing up. This is crucial. It is here that we can connect with the vulnerable, human side of these two people who later became our parents.

It is important to keep in mind that most often parents are flattered by their grown children asking them about their early lives. Unconsciously it is saying, "Dad, Mom, you are important to me not just as my parents, but as the human persons that you are." It pays tribute to their own roots. However, some parents, at first, put their grown children off with such statements as, "Oh, that's not important," "Why do you want to know about that?"

Often these put-off statements emanate from a certain shyness in the parents, or simply because this is a new experience for them. It is also important to be sensitive that our parents' childhoods could have been very painful or shameful to them. In these cases it may be very difficult for such parents to open up about their early lives. Or the parents may not feel very important about themselves and since such questions imply that they are important persons, such questions could be threatening.

I hope that the story of Jim Ryan encourages you, the reader, to embark upon a similar journey. It has the possibility of connecting you more deeply to your roots.

Chapter Fifteen

Underlying Dynamics
in Jim Ryan's Family

ॐ

FROM MY EXPERIENCE in helping people empower themselves, I have found several dynamics that seem to be basic and
pivotal in human behavior and human development. When we
see these dynamics working within a person we can better understand the human dimension of that person. Thus understanding
these few dynamics and how they function can help us understand our parents, grandparents, aunts, and uncles — our family
roots.

These dynamics were functioning beneath the behavior of Jim
Ryan's father, Sean, his grandparents, James and Margaret, and
within Jim himself. I will list these dynamics and give some examples of how they played a role in this family and helped Jim and
me understand how human and vulnerable these people were.
Understanding these dynamics allowed Jim to empathize with
his mother and father and grandparents. With this compassion,
Jim could more easily accept his roots as part of himself. Thus Jim
felt more together and complete. He felt stronger and had greater
confidence in himself. He had a greater sense of who he was. Jim
Ryan's self-esteem expanded.

Of all the dynamics at work within each human being, I believe
that there are six core dynamics that play a critical part in every

person's life and in every family. If one is a parent, then I add a seventh dynamic.

1. The *drive to have high self-esteem,* to feel good about oneself, to be at peace.

2. The *drive* to make sense, *to make meaning* out of life and life's events, *which meaning triggers an automatic emotional response.*

3. The *drive to survive when threatened* by using *coping strategies.*

4. The *urge to live by the rules* of one's life.

5. The *compelling wish to have good parents.*

6. The *drive to connect with others,* to relate to others for our survival and for our human fulfillment.

7. If we are parents, the *compelling wish to be good parents.*

Let me give a few examples of how these dynamics were at work in Jim Ryan's story. In the next chapter I will explain these dynamics in fuller detail and help you use them in understanding your parents as well as other significant members of your family.

Jim Ryan's journey began because he paid attention to a feeling he had, namely, the feeling of unrest. He shared that feeling with me, and I knew it came from a meaning he was giving to a life event. So I worked with Jim, trying to uncover the meaning that was triggering this feeling of unrest. It was not his current family life or professional career. When I discovered that his mother died when he was four and he knew little of her, I suggested that perhaps that was behind the unrest. A part of him was missing, and on some level he knew that he was not complete. I suggested that he deal with this issue to see if it was indeed the trigger. So by utilizing the second dynamic, meanings that trigger feelings, Jim began a journey that eventually led him to understand and appreciate how truly human his mother and father were.

Jim's unrest swelled into a dissatisfaction with himself. He was not upset with his wife and children, boss, or fellow workers. There was something about himself that he did not like. His self-esteem (the first dynamic) was being affected. He was disconnected from part of his roots, his mother. Thus he was cut off from himself, as his mother was part of him. His connection to his

father was lacking. He had serious puzzles about his father in re-
lation to his mother and he lacked information about his father's
early childhood.

Jim needed to be more integrated with his roots to feel a greater
sense of himself and to increase his self-worth.

When Jim visited his father he was confirmed in his suspicion
that the reason that his father did not talk about his mother was
his father's fear of upsetting Anna. So Jim could understand and
appreciate that his father was threatened (third dynamic). To cope
with the threat he remained silent about Bridget. Sean was also
threatened by the prospect that Jim might be adversely affected
if Anna became upset by discussions of Bridget in the house.
Silence was Sean's coping strategy.

Jim deepens his human connection to his father as Sean reveals his anguish in breaking an unconscious rule of his, namely,
"you must never upset your parents" (the fourth dynamic). That
hidden rule was violated when Sean let the dog out of the house
and the dog was killed by a car. Sean's father was extremely upset and blamed Sean's mother for being irresponsible in watching
over Sean. That episode only deepened the rule within Sean, as
he tells Jim, "I guess from that time on I was very careful not to
upset my parents."

The compelling wish to have good parents (fifth dynamic) begins to appear when Sean, ever so slightly, complains about his
mother getting on him for his grades in math, chemistry, and
physics. Sean was too obsessed with the rule to be a good boy to
get in touch with the fact that he really did want his mother to
respect his uniqueness and not try to make him like his brothers.
"I don't know why mother was such a stickler about math."

Later, Jim is able to appreciate how that nonacceptance by his
mother affected Sean more seriously than Sean himself appreciated. Jim was also able to understand how his grandmother,
Margaret, was only coping with the threat of the Depression,
and more importantly, fearing that Sean, like his father, would
be unfulfilled.

The sixth dynamic, the need to be connected, the need to relate
well to one another in the family, is operating throughout the
entire story of Jim Ryan. It was the lack of connection between
Jim and his mother that caused the restlessness within Jim. The
urge to be connected laid dormant, as it were, for years within

him. It then forced itself into his consciousness at this stage of his life.

Not only can we see the presence of this drive to be connected throughout Jim's story, but we can get clues to the operation of other dynamics by observing how the relating is going on. For example, the way Sean's mother was relating to Sean over his poor math and science grades indicated the presence of a threat in her. She coped with that threat by pestering Sean about his grades. So the prickly connection between Margaret and Sean revealed the presence of the third dynamic, the drive to cope when being threatened.

This example also reveals the presence of the seventh dynamic, the compelling wish to be good parents. Sean's uncle and father were not bothering him about the grades, but his mother was. His mother was assigning a particular meaning to Sean's poor showing in math and science. This meaning triggered the feeling of fear. But what added to the threat was the need for Margaret to be a good parent. Her self-esteem as a mother was at stake. If she didn't "save" Sean, she would not be a good parent in her own eyes. This intensified her pestering Sean about his grades. Apparently Sean's father did not assign the same meaning to Sean's weak math and science skills and therefore was not threatened. Sean's uncle, even if he had the same meaning as Margaret's, would not have been bothered since he was not the parent.

These are a few examples of the core dynamics operating in Jim Ryan's story. The dynamics emerge as Sean reveals his life to Jim. It is easy to see how the functioning of these dynamics affected the way everyone related in the family.

I think that you can see how understanding these core dynamics was guiding me in helping Jim and in enabling Jim to make sense of his father and mother and grandparents. The more Jim understood his parents and grandparents, the more he could empathize with them. His compassion for his own family members grew. As that compassion increased, Jim was feeling more deeply bonded to his roots on the basis of their shared humanity. Jim was seeing Sean as Sean rather than as father; Bridget as Bridget rather than just mother. Jim was taking a safe journey to meet his parents and members of his family, his roots, as human!

Chapter Sixteen

Application of the Dynamics to Your Family

❧

I WANT TO EXPLAIN in greater detail the meaning of these core dynamics and how they work in human behavior. Then I will invite you to take some time to reflect on how these dynamics may have worked, and may still be working, in the lives of your parents. Familiarizing yourself with how they operated in your parents will allow you to see how they may operate in other important members of your family of origin. This will give you a deeper understanding of these significant people in your family roots. It will aid you in perceiving them as human, equal to you, instead of perceiving them in the roles they played as parent, aunt, uncle, grandparent. You will then be able to accept them as they really are, as they fully are in their rich and vulnerable humanity. You will be filling yourself up with your roots.

Dynamic #1: The drive to have high self-esteem

We have often heard that the most basic human drive is to survive. It is this life force to survive that is so powerful in the tiny infant. Often, against life-threatening odds, the baby will cling to life in a way that is amazing. The psychological drive to survive is just as important and as powerful as is the biological instinct to survive.

This psychological drive is not about "Will I live?" but about "Am I worthwhile, important, lovable, likeable?" It is about self-esteem. This core psychological component drives me to feel happy and good about myself. Psychological survival is to be secure in my emotional and mental well-being. Both the physical and psychological drives to survive operate deeply throughout our lifetime. The unconscious physical instinct to survive is what makes us duck when our head is about to bump into a low-hanging branch of a tree; the unconscious psychological drive to survive is what makes us twinge inside when we feel someone doesn't like us.

I teach a course at the University of Oklahoma on family systems. The graduate students range in age from twenty-four to sixty-five. After we get acquainted with each other, I do an opening exercise, and I always get the same results. I have them stand in a circle and I tell them to look around the circle and to pick someone they know the least. They do this without speaking. Then I tell them to move to get with their partner and to sit down opposite each other, closing their eyes. All of this is done nonverbally. With their eyes closed I invite them to be aware of what they are thinking and feeling. When they report their experience, over half the class reports feeling nervous, anxious, afraid. These feelings flow from such thoughts as, "Will I be chosen?" "Will I be rejected if I choose someone?" "Will I be the last one chosen?" (i.e., what's wrong with me), "Will my partner like me?" All these questions involve one's lovability, self-worth. That self-esteem, good feeling about oneself, is being threatened by this simple exercise. This exercise reveals how the instinct to survive psychologically lies deep inside each of us. It is always there. No matter how strong we are, how good we feel about ourselves, that high self-esteem can be threatened. When it is threatened on the simplest level, we feel nervous, anxious, fearful.

I believe that this drive to feel good about ourselves is as powerful as the drive to survive physically. It is certainly the main preoccupation of our maturing life once our physical survival is secured. It is the determining factor of all we do. The question of what will make us happy invisibly guides our daily life. Unhappiness, unrest, feeling out of sorts, feeling bad about ourselves tell us that something is wrong with our lives. The drive to high self-esteem is the deep and unconscious gyroscope of our actions and being. This core dynamic explains much about our own human behavior as well as that of our mothers and fathers.

Dynamic #2: The drive to make meaning, which meaning triggers emotions

The second central dynamic drives us to make sense out of our lives. This dynamic results in a set of meanings about life, events, and reality that we learn as we grow up. Most of these meanings are learned rather than genetically given. The basic meanings of what is love, what is a man, a woman, husband, wife, mother, father, what makes for happiness, what is good and bad, how should children be raised, who or what is God, what is safe or dangerous, what is the purpose of life, what is honorable and dishonorable, true or false, what is patriotic, healthy and un-healthy — all these meanings are learned most often within the families and homes we are raised in. They may be transformed or changed as we mature, but they begin at home.

These meanings are connected to emotions. That is, whenever we have an emotion such as sadness, anger, joy, or thrill, it is usu-ally, if not always, attached to some meaning we are making of what is happening. For example, if I am sixteen and my mother dies, I might feel extremely sad for I see in this death the *loss* of my closest support, my nurturing mother. If I also see in this death the loss of the only one who really cares about me in the world, then I will feel panic, for who now will care for me? If I interpret this death as God taking my mother from me, I might feel angry toward God, or I'll feel a generalized anger and re-sentment. If I assign a further meaning to this death, namely, that my father was responsible for her death because he tormented her, I'll feel angry at him. If I see no way out for my future, I'll despair.

On the other hand, if I see my mother as a dominating ogre, a persistent roadblock to what I want to do and be in life, then I may feel some relief. If I have a meaning that it is wrong to feel relief at the death of my mother, I'll feel guilty.

If I have a meaning about God, such as God knows best, loves my mother, and loves me and will take care of me, then my feelings about the loss are not so acute.

There are two things about emotions that are very important to know. One, these emotions are natural, biological reactions to the meanings or sense we make out of events. They are part of our genetic makeup as human beings in the sense that our mind and body are integrated. *Therefore, there is no feeling or emotion that is wrong or bad.* To tell a child, or myself, not to fear, don't be angry, don't cry, is tantamount to saying that we should not be what we are. These messages are extremely nonvalidating. They connote, "Don't be." What might be wrong or bad or inappropriate is the *meaning* that I am assigning to the event that automatically triggers the natural emotion. So the message I might give to a child or myself is about the *meaning* I am making out of the event. For example, I might think it through and begin to see that my mother is not the only one who can take care of me. I am now sixteen and can fend for myself. I have other relatives and friends who will help me. As my meaning shifts so does the emotion shift. So my panic will be less intense.

The second thing so important about emotions is that feelings can lead us to understand others. Since the emotion comes from a meaning, the emotion can suggest what is going on deeply within a person. Take the case of the death of my mother. If I begin to crumble and become nonfunctional due to the panic I am experiencing, someone, say my aunt, may be wise enough to see that my behavior is an expression of my panic. Then my aunt might begin to ponder, why is Bill so frightened? Perhaps my aunt talks to me, trying to figure out what is going on that scares me so. As she begins to uncover the meaning triggering the panic, namely, that no one will take care of me, she can help me see how that meaning does not fit reality.

Pause for a moment to consider a puzzle you may have about one of your parents. For example, perhaps you wonder why your father was so angry at the kids, his wife, and the world. His anger seemed to be always beneath the surface and often the intensity of the anger was not in proportion to what was going on. So your puzzle is about the very presence of a feeling. What is the meaning that Dad is making that triggers this irrational anger; what meaning is keeping his anger there beneath the surface? Since nothing in the immediate environment makes any sense as a cause for this kind of anger, perhaps it was a meaning developed in his childhood.

As you reflect upon the way he grew up, it dawns on you that he was the second son and that all of his parent's attention, approval, and adulation went to the first son. Your dad felt slighted, less than his brother, and put down. He struggled to gain some recognition and acceptance, but never got it. Not having this primary need met, your father grew angry. The understandable meaning he had was that "I deserve and need love and acceptance from my parents; they are refusing me; I'm not getting this need met anywhere." This meaning triggers anger. Anger is his emotional response to not getting what he wants and needs. This anger becomes part of your father's makeup, a style of life as it were. This anger drives people away. Your mother saw something else in your father that attracted her to marrying him. But soon the anger got to her and she too withdrew and found it difficult to accept him. So for all practical purposes, your father's normal childhood response of anger keeps him from satisfying his need to be accepted, even in his adult years.

This example gives you an idea of how to proceed. So now consider some puzzle you have about one of your parents. Notice what feeling your parent manifests that is connected to that which puzzles you. It might be a listlessness or an unrest or chronic anger or excitement. What do you think is the meaning that your parent is making that explains that emotion? Think of several meanings. Which one seems to fit best? Your answer is only your assumption. Only your parent knows the correct meaning. However, if you have never tried to go from the emotion to the meaning before, you may begin to see more of the human dynamic working in your parent, which then allows you to see the person as more human. When there is a feeling that a person persistently carries around, often the meaning triggering that feeling stems from early childhood.

Emotions are the key or entrée to a person's set of meanings about life. They help us make sense of the person. This is one of the reasons why therapists spend so much time dealing with the emotions of a person who comes for help. It is not just to encourage a person to express feelings, but it is to understand the depth of the person. This drive to make sense out of things is a core dynamic because it goes to the core of our nature as human beings. We are rational animals. Being intelligent animals, we are thinkers and feelers. So the most normal way for us to behave is to figure things out; since we are animals we also have an integrated emotional response to our thoughts.

Dynamic #3: The drive to survive by coping with threats

The third central human dynamic I have found is connected to our primal instinct to survive physically and psychologically. Whenever our physical life or self-esteem is threatened, we automatically respond to protect our life and mental well-being. These responses are often called coping strategies or mechanisms. Much of the behavior that causes trouble for ourselves and others is this response in trying to protect ourselves. Some call it "acting out." For example, whenever I get grumpy and irritable, it is usually in response to my not feeling good about myself. I am not happy for one reason or another. My self-worth is being threatened on some level. I may not know what it is at the time. But usually I feel I am being thwarted or unable to achieve what I want that seems good to me. Now whether or not my meaning is based on reality is another matter. The fact is that I am interpreting what is going on in my life at the time as inimical to my happiness. I am feeling threatened. So I protect myself by thrashing around irritably. This way of coping defends me by driving away those around me. When I am alone I can put myself back together, get my bearings, find myself, and get on with the task. Or the frustration builds to a point where I gather enough steam to move toward my goal.

This way to cope has its advantages and disadvantages. The advantages I have just described. The disadvantage is that it makes people upset with me. This sets off another threat: "My loved ones don't love me." Now I have to cope with that threat!

Consider other coping behavior. What explains the rebellion of teenagers? What is going on when children misbehave when their parents begin to divorce? What explains the sudden eruption of violence at the Rodney King acquittal in May 1992? Behind each of these acts is the fact that in some way the persons feel threatened because of the meaning they have given to the situation.

The children who begin to fail in school, disobey, grow sullen during the divorce of their parents are obviously threatened by the breakup of the family. They can be threatened on many levels: "What will happen to me?" "Who will care for me?" "Am

I responsible for this divorce?" "Am I a failure for not keeping the marriage together?" So the children's acting out is a scream for help. It is their unconscious way to try to protect themselves from however they are experiencing the threat emanating from the divorce of their parents.

There are several important aspects to keep in mind about this human dynamic of being threatened and coping. The first is that, as with emotions in general, the feeling of threat, fear, or anxiety, is a natural result of the meaning a person assigns to what is happening.

Second, being threatened is a normal, expected occurrence, since every human being is a limited and vulnerable creature. As such our life and self-esteem are not permanently secured. If we were limitless, as God is described, we would never experience threat since our life would be immortal and our self-esteem perfect. But we are not God, and thus we are rendered vulnerable by our limitations.

Third, to cope, to defend ourselves, flows directly from our drive to survive as humans, so it too is a normal human response.

Fourth, these ways to protect ourselves are learned from early on. For example, violence is being used more and more as a way to cope, especially by youngsters. Where are they learning this method? From home and now from television.

The most important aspect of this human dynamic is that it is precisely in these moments of threat and coping that we have a wonderful opportunity to grow humanly and spiritually. Usually we view being threatened and the more common ways of coping with threat as a negative experience. As a result, many try to arrange their lives to avoid these threats as much as possible. An example of this is the various cosmetic efforts people undertake to avoid the thought and reality of death. However, dealing with threatening experiences in a positive manner can be the very way to expand our boundaries, to reach a higher level of human existence.

Let me explain how this is so. Not all coping is a negative acting out. There is a way to protect oneself from being threatened that is positive. It enhances the lives of the person being threatened and of the persons involved in the threatening situation. It respects the context that these people are in. These strategies take into account and respect the reality of self, others, and the environment. The result is a win-win outcome rather than a win-lose outcome, which the negative coping methods produce.

For example, a better way for me to cope with my situation above is quickly to become aware of my feeling grumpy and irritable. Realizing I am irritable rings a bell. I ask myself, What is this all about? When I try to deal with the reality of my *feelings* and the *meaning* that triggers those feelings, I may discover that I need some time by myself. I begin to see that I need to do some things that I know will make me feel better about myself, such as being creative or helping others. So instead of continuing the irritable behavior, I can let my needs be known to those around me, asking them to respect those needs. Instead of driving them away, I invite them to help me. This, more often than not, elicits from them a willingness to cooperate. As I seek time alone or some creative activity, they understand what I am doing and feel good about being a part of it. As a result, I am feeling better about myself and so are those around me. Furthermore, I am not disrupting the context of my life. Indeed I am adding to it by being creative.

Now how does this simple example illustrate any human or spiritual growth on my part? This realistic way of coping demands that I *develop the human skill* to be aware of my feelings as soon as possible (something not always easily done). It demands that I *be responsible* for both my feelings and the meaning that triggers these feelings. It means that I can't go around blaming others for my misery or for feeling threatened. While others or the context can be involved as the stimulus of the threat, it is *my* meaning that I assign to the event that makes me feel threatened. Since I am the one feeling threatened, it is up to me to take *the first steps* to remedy the situation. This way of coping demands again that I be responsible. It demands that *I risk* putting myself forward by expressing what is going on with me and what my needs are. By doing this I risk being ignored, put down, rejected, or refused. That is, I risk being hurt. Taking such risks demands *courage.* If I am contemned by those involved, I must then deal with that hurt and the meaning behind it. So that means I must go to another level with this issue. It means that *I must take further responsibility* for myself and perhaps even *risk* more, which demands *more courage and discipline* from me.

I hope that you can see how in such a simple little human encounter personal growth can be achieved. If this is so with a threat so small that it triggers grumpiness, how much more growth is imbedded in the more powerful threats that we encounter in life. This is why death itself contains within it such a momentous opportunity for spiritual growth. I will treat this more fully in a chapter later in the book.

I invite you to think of one of your parents whose behavior has bothered you. Examine that behavior. Now try to figure out what it might be that is threatening your parent. Is it something that you are doing? Or is your parent threatened by some other aspect of life and you just happen to be the recipient of that negative behavior? Is your parent threatened by something going back to early childhood?

See if you can trace where your parent learned that way of coping with threat. What keeps your parent from using a more real, adequate, and positive way of coping? As you ponder these questions, perhaps you can understand your parent better. Perhaps, you can appreciate that person as being human rather than just as your parent bothering you. If so, this does not imply that you must let yourself be poorly treated by your parent. Fully understanding your parent is one thing; protecting yourself is another. Both can be done. *In fact by understanding your parent accurately gives you better ways to protect yourself.*

Dynamic #4: The urge to live by the rules of one's life

The fourth important dynamic of our personality is a set of internal rules that governs our life. These rules lie deep in our unconscious and are always operating. They are learned, and most of them were learned at home. These rules also flow from meanings we have about life. For example, the rule "obey your parents" flows from our meaning of parents as those who know best for us. The rules can also take on the form of a meaning we make of something. For instance, the rule to obey parents forms part of the meaning of what it takes to be a good boy or girl. That is, a good child is one who obeys.

Many of these rules are passed on from generation to generation and enter into the larger culture of clan, race, or nation. Once this happens, then the culture carries the rules and helps families reinforce the rules with their offspring. For example, the patriotic rule "you must serve your country in war" is certainly taught at home, but it is powerfully reinforced by the national culture. So much so that parents who teach pacifism to their children risk being labeled unpatriotic or an enemy of the state.

Some examples of these rules of life are: Be perfect, never fail, do the best you can, never dishonor your parents, don't hurt others, play it safe, take chances, never tell family secrets, be like me, don't cry, don't be afraid, enjoy life, spend it while you got it (a rule the current economic culture of easy credit reinforces), save for a rainy day, live for the moment, do unto others before they do unto you, do unto others as you would have them do to you, be seen and not heard, make others happy, beware of others, be competitive, be cooperative, be in control, work hard.

These rules for the most part are incorporated into our psychic system unconsciously by the way events occur and by the behavior of others, especially those in power over us as our parents. For example, the economic depression of the 1930s was an event whereby many adopted the rule "save for a rainy day," or "live frugally." As a result many people today are well off but live in a miserly fashion. Another example would be that of two teenagers carried away with sexual passion who are now responsible for a pregnancy. Under the guidance of their parents, they give the baby for adoption. The adopted child may grow up with a primal fear of rejection and forms a rule "never trust others," which is also a coping strategy. These are two examples of how events lead a person to make rules. An illustration of how the example of others inculcates a rule is that of two parents who never argue before their child. The child learns "never fight your spouse."

Some rules are more powerful than others. The rules that are more deeply entrenched and thus harder to break or change are those that have the most severe sanctions attached to them. The adopted person's rule, "don't trust others," is powerful because of the sanction embedded in the adoption experience. It is as if to say, "If you trust others, you will be severely hurt by rejection again; therefore protect yourself by not trusting."

The child whose parents never fought learns the rule not to fight one's spouse. However, that rule will be more powerful if one day the parents do fight and soon they divorce. The child learns the sanction: If you fight your marriage will end. This drastic sanction makes this rule very strict and powerful. The child, now grown and married, will abide by this rule out of fear of the marriage ending. So the married person avoids conflict at all costs, one of which is to suppress needs and wants.

There are several important considerations about the presence of these sets of rules imbedded in each human being. First, most rules are very functional. They have been tested by years of experience and are helpful in living lives of high self-esteem. Many are not so helpful. Rules that contain "never" or "always" can become unreasonable at times. However, a rule that embraces the "never" or "always" tends to be more powerful. "Never make a mistake" is stronger than "try not to err" or "learn from your mistakes."

Second, as with meanings, since rules are learned, they can be changed, although at times with great difficulty.

Third, the presence of powerful rules can create threatening situations for us. For example, I can be terribly threatened if I am about to tell a friend a family secret when I have a rule never to do this. The unconscious threat is that if I tell this secret, my parents will not approve of me or will not love me. I may be fifty years old and on the surface that threat is ridiculous, but it functions as if I am nine years old and still at home!

Fourth, these rules are so much a part of our personality that to violate one is like violating oneself. Therefore when such a rule is broken, self-worth collapses. For example, "be perfect" is a rule that was powerfully implanted in me. I have spent years trying to change that rule to a more realistic one. While I have made progress in transforming it, I can still be very upset at times when I make a mistake.

Adopting a set of powerful rules in our lives and living by them is a core dynamic because again it is based on a fundamental aspect of our human nature. We are intelligent and *free*. We see and can make choices between alternatives. Our lives are not completely guided by a set of rules bestowed upon us in our instincts. So we are free to decide upon rules that we judge will be beneficial for our survival and happiness. In fact, we must decide upon many rules that facilitate the flow of our lives. If we fail to do so, we live in chaos, confusion, and danger. A traffic rule is a good example. In the United States we have decided to drive on the right side of the road; in Britain they have decided to drive on the left side. We think through our rules, design them, change them whenever appropriate. Our rules are freely made, and as we mature we have the freedom to abide by these early learned rules or not. We have the freedom to change our internal rules, even though at times it is difficult.

Now try to identify a few powerful rules of each of your parents. What would happen to them if they broke or came close to breaking one of these rules? How would they react to you if you broke the rule? Try to imagine how they learned these rules. Identify a powerful rule that you have that you deem not very helpful, at least at times. What happens when you break the rule?

From this reflection, perhaps you have a deeper understanding of how breaking those rules was so threatening to your parents. Perhaps you can now see your parents more as humans than as parents.

Dynamic #5: The compelling wish to have good parents

Over the years I have become aware that what I once regarded as a simple cliché is indeed a most profound truth that has enormous impact on all of us, namely, that every person wants a good mommy and daddy. While that is a simple enough truth, the depth of that reality has been reinforced in me in the last fifteen years as I have helped people reconnect with their family roots. This, what I consider to be the fifth core human dynamic, is absolutely crucial to each of us. I have seen this dynamic continue to drive people to change their parents even though the person is sixty years old and the parent is eighty-two. The sixty-year-old still wants that parent to be the kind of parent the sixty-year-old thinks that parent ought to be. The most consistent and basic demand is to have our parents approve and accept us.

This psychological drive to have functional, decent, honorable parents is what also causes many to cut themselves off from their parents when they judge that their parents have miserably failed them. Their hurt and lack of fulfillment can be so deep, so primal, that the cutting off is a way to protect themselves from the pain. They can cut themselves off by maintaining an intense anger toward their parents, or by having nothing to do with them and telling themselves that they have no need of their parents. They create a mental state that eliminates their parents from their lives, as if they do not exist and never did. Yet, as we have seen earlier, our parents are part of us for better or worse.

I have come to see how important this fundamental craving to have good parents is. As I have said, it is so important that we can exert years of enormous energy trying to shape up our mother or father. Or we can expend great unconscious energy pretending they don't count or don't exist. The reason, I think, that this is so important, long after a child is grown, is not just that a child needs the nurturance and protection of parents for survival. It is not just that a child carries scars of an abused childhood into adult life. It is not just because the child has learned some dysfunctional pattern from them. It is not just that the adult is still suffering some of the unmet needs of childhood, like the need for closeness and security. No, the craving, the demand, for parents to be good is important simply because *these parents are part of me.* I actually have their chromosomes; I carry some of their body and mind in me. If the parents are damaged, I am damaged. I have come to believe that this reality of being one with one's roots lies in the deepest unconscious part of a person. *This above all is what creates shame.* The shame and embarrassment flowing from this is more fundamental than any shame that results from individual acts such as physical or sexual abuse, alcoholic episodes, or criminal acts. The individual acts, shameful as they are in themselves, point toward the deeper reality and resulting shame, namely, "I have damaged, sick, weak, warped, corrupted parents (and they are part of me)." The shame is so intense that those who have such parents cannot share that with anyone. They keep it inside secretly — or, at least, they try to. After the child has grown, it is not the fear of the parent that renders the person silent; it is the shame. "That parent is part of me; I'm too embarrassed to admit it, even to myself."

How often I have seen people deny to themselves that one or both of their parents were alcoholic or abusive. How many deny that they even had a painful childhood! Their shame drives them to concoct a fantasy that their lives and parents are normal.

While that shame is present, there is no hope for such people to accept their roots as part of themselves. But I have seen so many people find relief when they can finally admit to themselves and to others that indeed their parents were severely lacking. When this happens, then these persons take the next step and begin to discover the human, vulnerable persons behind the failures and abusive actions. They realize that these persons came into the world wanting love, attention, nurturance, understanding, affection, and acceptance. But these future parents, too, had a difficult family life and in order to cope with their pain and threat resorted to inhuman means. When the future mother and father dated each other, they began to hope that something decent could happen to them. Unfortunately they were not mature enough to deal with the stresses of early marriage and parenthood, and when their lives began to fall apart, they took to drugs, abusive behavior, harshness, abandonment. When a person understands that about these parents, then that person can accept them, not as parents, i.e., in the role they played, but as humans who were themselves damaged early in their lives. When these two humans are accepted as human, the person becomes whole because that person has finally said yes to that very important part of self, one's roots.

Dynamic #6: The drive to connect with others

Much, if not most, of our human activity is engaged in an enterprise that can be labelled "getting bonded or connected to another." If we took an average day of our life and did a time analysis, mental process analysis, and activity analysis of that day, we could see how much energy is spent relating to other human beings. Even the person who is isolated, friendless, without family, can spend the entire day coping with his or her lack of human connection. In effect, this lonely person spends most of her or his energies in dealing with relationships, i.e., how to gain one or how to deal with the pain of their absence.

There is much at stake in being properly connected to other humans. Earlier I described how crucial it is for the child to be properly bonded to parents. It is from this appropriate bonding that a child's physical and psychological life is secured. If the bonding is poorly done, if the relating is inappropriate, then the child can be severely hurt. The children who cannot bond with their fathers or mothers because they are simply not there will carry those scars into adulthood.

There is more at stake in being connected to others than mere physical and mental survival. No matter how mature and independent we are as adults, we are still dependent creatures needing others. We move from being dependent in childhood to being interdependent in adulthood. Again this interdependence is needed for our well-being. We may need a doctor to stay alive; we need a friend, a loved one, to feel good about ourselves.

The enhancement of our lives depends upon how well, how intimately we can relate to others. The millionaire who has no close friends is poverty stricken. It is through intimacy that two people give themselves to each other so that each person walks away with the other inside in some real sense.

The best kind of relating involves all parts of us, the physical, the mental, and the spiritual. Too often relating is done just on an intellectual level, with little sharing of touching, affection, and emotions.

Freeman Dyson in his book *Weapons and Hope* (New York: Harper & Row, 1984) comments on how often war is appealing to men because it is a context in which permission and encouragement is given for men to bind together emotionally and physically. For example, men hold and cradle each other when wounded, struggling to survive in life-and-death situations. They depend on each other for their very lives. They use their minds, their senses, their emotions, their bodies to help each other. While war is hell, it is also a peak human experience in the sense that men are challenged to use their capacities in common bond with others to stay alive.

Perhaps this explains why some veterans love to gather in reunions to retell their war experiences. Some never bond with others as closely as they did with their comrades on the field of battle.

Not only is the drive to be deeply connected to others a core human dynamic, but achieving that goal is profoundly affected by the first five dynamics I have described and the way we relate in turn affects these five dynamics. Let me give an example of this interconnection, and then I will describe the significance of this in understanding the humanness of our parents and members of our family roots.

From what I wrote in chapter 7, you can see that the way parents relate to each other and to their children influences the self-esteem of the children. This also influences the self-esteem of the parents! If the parents relate poorly to the children and the children begin to feel bad about themselves, the parents will recognize this and will begin to feel bad about themselves.

Inappropriate relating cannot only threaten others, but it can also teach inadequate coping strategies. As a parent, if I respond to being threatened by blaming others, never taking any responsibility myself for what is happening, I teach my children that blaming is the way to defend oneself when threatened.

If I relate to my wife by ignoring or not trying to understand her, she can be threatened and will resort to some sort of self-defense. She can withdraw, or give in, or attack, or be distractive. Or she can try to deal realistically and openly with her feelings and needs and with my feelings and needs. So the way we relate to others can both threaten others and teach coping strategies.

The way we relate to others can teach rules, or violate rules, or comply with rules. I gave an example earlier of how a child was taught the rule never to argue with a spouse from the way the parents related to each other.

The need to have good parents is also affected by the way we relate. Let us say that you, my teacher, remind me of my father who consistently ignored me. I am not consciously aware of this. If you do something that I think is ignoring me, the sting of being ignored by you, who are my teacher, an authority figure, is magnified by my hanging my father's hat on you. So I intensify my effort to get you to pay attention to me. You on the other hand (to complicate the scenario) are fed up with your kids bugging you for attention. So as I double my effort to get you to attend to me, you ignore me all the more. The harder I work, the more you ignore me.

From this example you can see how the way the teacher relates to me awakens my unfulfilled need to have a father who pays attention to me. This in turn influences the way I relate to this teacher.

So the way others relate to us influences these five dynamics. On the other hand, these dynamics profoundly influence the way we relate. For example, breaking the rule "never hurt others," may so threaten me that I may withdraw from the one I have offended rather than apologize. I may be so absorbed by my own negative feelings that I am not able at the moment to own up to my mistake and apologize. Part of the meaning I attach to hurting someone, especially a woman, is that she will not love me and approve of me. This in turn deepens my withdrawal. Then my self-esteem is lowered. This will make it even more difficult for me to mend the relationship.

This exemplifies how the five dynamics influence the way a person relates to another. I have chosen negative examples here. Positive examples would show how these five core dynamics influence how we relate in a positive way.

The point of all this in terms of our endeavor in this book is that the interconnection of these six dynamics (the drive toward self-esteem, making meanings that trigger emotions, coping strategies, rules of life, the need for good parents, the need to be connected) offers great help in understanding the human character of our parents. Because of the intimate connection between these dynamics, we can use the "need to be connected" drive to see how the other five dynamics are functioning in members of our family. So if we examine the way the members of our family relate to each other, to friends, and to the world, we can achieve a more thorough understanding of how indeed our parents function. This will lead us to see that indeed they are as human as I am.

I would like to show you an example of how this can be done from my own life. In my mother's eyes, her mother could do no wrong. In fact, my mother used to say that grandmother was a saint. (I happened to agree with that opinion too, but I had the advantage of being with my grandmother after she had accumulated some sixty years of wisdom and maturity from dealing with seven children and her rapidly changing world. I doubt if grandmother was a saint at thirty when my mother was eight years old.) My mother related to her mother with great respect and deference. She related to her as her ideal.

The meaning of being a "saint" in my mother's eyes was that her mother was a highly moral, religious person devoted to her Catholicism, as well as being an extremely practical housewife, cook, baker, seamstress, quilter, and a firm and loving mother.

Understanding how my mother idealized and sanctified her mother allowed me to understand the terrible feelings of guilt my mother had whenever she broke one of the church's laws. I'll never forget how shocked I was when, traveling with her in Europe, she lost track of the days and ate meat on Friday. Later that day, when she discovered it was Friday, she was extremely upset.

She bemoaned the fact for several days, and was very anxious to go to confession. I couldn't believe it. Even the church taught that if you forget what day it is, you are not breaking the law of abstinence. As reasonable as that is, Mother was not influenced by such logic. She should not have forgotten what day it was! What was at stake was not so much breaking a law of the church or forgetting the day, but it was violating her own mother's principles. What would her mother think of her (even though she was dead)!

This dynamic helped me to understand that when Mother complained to me on occasions that "I'll never be as good as your grandmother," she was deadly serious. This perception of herself as not being as good as her mother lowered my mother's self-esteem.

Understanding this relationship between my mother and her mother helps me to make sense of other behaviors of my mother that had eluded me till I grasped the significance of this relationship.

At this point, I invite you to pause for a moment to consider how your father related to your mother, and how she related to him. How did each parent relate to his and her parents? As you consider this, what does it say to you about their meanings, and rules, what threatened them and how they coped? Does it open up to you any understanding of the deeper dynamics working in each of your parents?

Dynamic #7: The drive to be good parents

Once a person becomes a parent, the drive to be a good parent comes into focus. Over the years, I have come to appreciate how powerful and significant this drive is.

It is this need to be a good parent that can make parents feel guilty when they perceive that they have failed in this task. It is this drive that threatens a parent if the child fails to respond to the parent's effort. When the threat is severe, it triggers a near panic response and, most often, an unproductive coping mechanism. This panic inhibits a calm, reasoned, sensible response. One's resources are not available due to the intensity of the fear or threat.

It is this drive that propels parents to try to make their children be what the parents believe is a "good child." Often this effort blinds the parent from studying the child, so as to learn from the child what the child needs and wants. It is as if the prelearned and preconceived meaning of what a good child looks like becomes more important than being amenable to the uniqueness of the child. While our basic human needs are all the same, the ways they are met and nurtured can be manifold. What may fit for one child does not for another. In spite of this, the drive to be the perfect parent can still move the parent to rely more on the map of how everything *should* be rather than allowing for the uniqueness of the child.

It is this drive to be perfect parents that drives parents to have perfect children!

It is this drive that can create in some parents fear and feelings of terrible inadequacies.

It is this drive that can make parents worry far too much about what others will think of the job they are doing.

It is this drive that makes some parents too possessive of their children, too cautious with them, too protective of them. This drive can make parents threatened by advice-giving grandparents, aunts, and uncles. It can propel parents to resist negative criticisms from relatives, friends, and teachers.

It is this drive that makes parents still try to govern their children even when they are forty years old!

This drive can also create low self-worth in parents if they see their children going wrong, at least in their eyes. Failure to be the good parent is taken as being a total failure at times. One's whole identity can be caught up in the job of parenting. So when that job is perceived as a failure, the parent can be crushed.

Again pause for a moment and consider your own folks. If you are a parent, you will be able to identify with what I have been saying. If not, assume the belief that your parents have this central core dynamic: to be good parents. See if that deepens your understanding of some of their behavior with you and your siblings. If you can see how this dynamic was working in them, perhaps you can appreciate how truly human and vulnerable they were or are.

Chapter Seventeen

Using Genograms, Chronologies, Birth Fantasies

✿

UP TO THIS POINT I have shown how conversing with relatives is the most common way to reconnect with one's roots. I have also described the core dynamics that operate in each of us that help us understand our parents and relatives in a human fashion. Now I want to discuss other methods that we can use to embark upon this safe journey to see our parents as adults, equal to us.

When I teach my graduate course at the university, the students are to present a paper in which they complete genograms, historical family chronologies, and birth fantasies of their mother, father, and themselves. In every class there are some students who report that in the very doing of the paper they began to understand their parents and grandparents in a new way. They claim that problems and puzzles they have had with these families were resolved. They talk about having feelings of relief, compassion, and closeness with their parents and grandparents. They see their parents more as being human than in the role of being parents.

I encourage you to undertake the work that I describe in this chapter. You too may profit as my students have.

As I begin to describe how to do these tasks, you will see immediately that to do a thorough job you will probably need to talk to your parents, aunts, uncles, and grandparents, if they are still alive. Later, I will offer some suggestions on how to do this without unduly threatening them, as some relatives may be threatened by being asked about their lives. These conversations, stimulated by gathering facts for the genograms and chronologies, often have the same quality as the conversation of Jim Ryan with his father, Sean. These conversations create a new connection with them resulting in a feeling of wholeness, a greater sense of self-identity, and increased confidence and self-esteem.

I have presented the genograms of Jim Ryan's family on page 51. Note the information on these genograms; names, birth and death dates of each person, marriage and divorce dates. We will start with this and add other information to the genograms (which is not included on Jim Ryan's genogram).

Let me walk you through this work. We begin with the genograms of your family of origin.

Put your father's full name in a rectangle and your mother's full name in a circle. All males are designated by rectangles and females by circles. Then draw lines and put in the children and dates as illustrated below. A solid line represents a marriage. If you parents were not married draw a dotted line. If you are adopted, the first genogram should be that of your biological parents. While there may be some resistance to doing this, it is critical that you do so because you carry within you the blending of the twenty-three chromosomes from each biological parent. It has been my experience that many adopted individuals have problems because

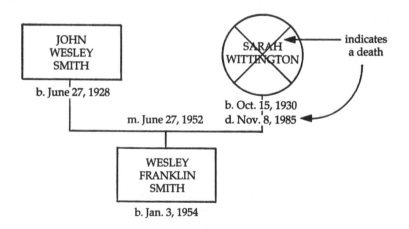

Wesley Franklin Smith's Family of Origin

they reject their biological parents, which is in a sense to reject a part of themselves. I will speak more about this in the next chapter.

If you do not know the names or dates of any of the persons in these genograms, it is important that you make up or guess the name or date. Putting a name and a birth date to a person in your lineage personifies the person. Leaving an empty rectangle or circle symbolizes that the person is nonexistent and has played no role in your life, when in reality each person in a family system has something to do with the outcome of that family. When you guess at a name or date, put a question mark beside it as below in the example of an adopted person.

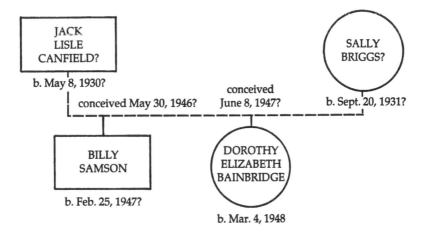

Dorothy Elizabeth Bainbridge's Biological Family of Origin

In the case of an adopted person, after the biological family is mapped in a genogram, proceed to do the adopted family of origin. In both the biological and adopted families make genograms for the paternal and maternal families. Again, in regard to the biological mother and father you will probably need to make up the maternal and paternal families of mother, father, and siblings. Set your fantasy powers free. Do not be inhibited by lack of actual knowledge.

Note that siblings are placed in the genogram from left to right in order of their births.

Some families are more complicated. I'll show you how to deal with some of the complications in the diagrams on pp. 96 and 97.

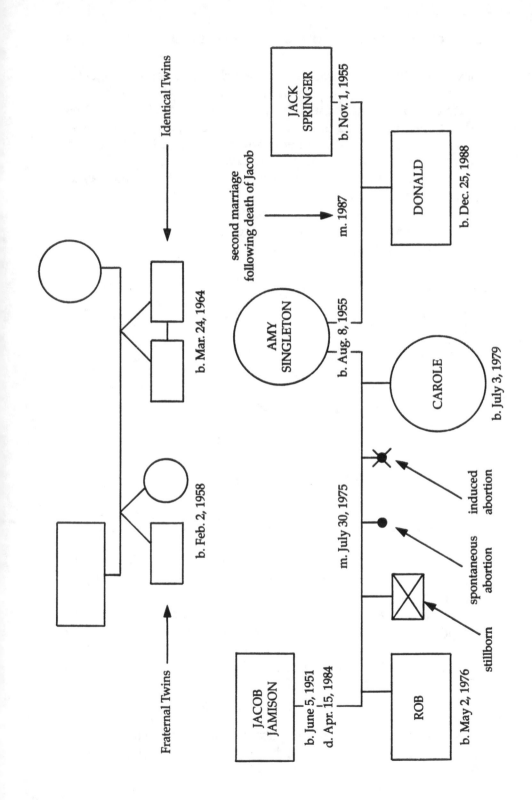

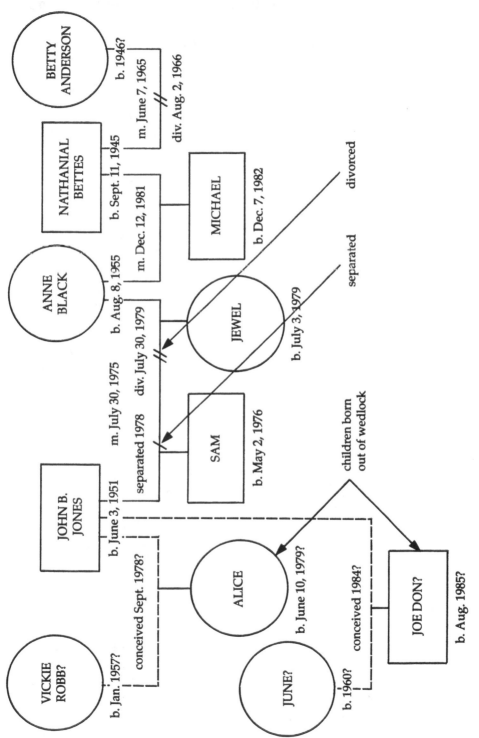

From these examples you can see how to draw other complicated systems. For example:

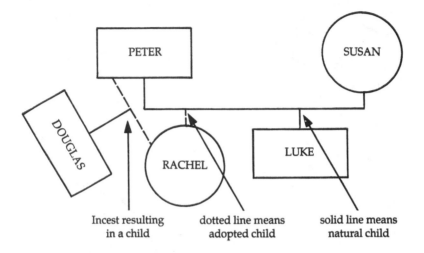

Incest resulting   dotted line means   solid line means
  in a child   adopted child   natural child

After you have made the genogram of your family of origin,
place under each name several adjectives or short phrases that
describe your perception of the personality of that person. Then
draw lines with arrows and put over the lines a statement reflecting your perception of how this person related to the other. On
the following page is an illustration of one complete genogram
of Wesley Franklin Smith.

Having completed the genogram of your family of origin,
write down what you are feeling and thinking.

Now do a genogram for your mother's family with the adjectives and lines of relationships, just as you did for your own
family. After doing this, again pause and be aware of what you
are feeling and thinking. Write down your reactions.

Now do your father's genogram as you did your maternal
family, again ending by writing down your feelings and thoughts.
Take a break if you have not already done so. Perhaps leave the
work alone for a day or two.

To bring fuller life to the genogram, the next task is to list
under the name of your father, mother, and yourself your perception of five of the seven core dynamics explained in chapters
15 and 16. I have deliberately chosen the word "perception" here
and above rather than saying "write adjectives or short phrases

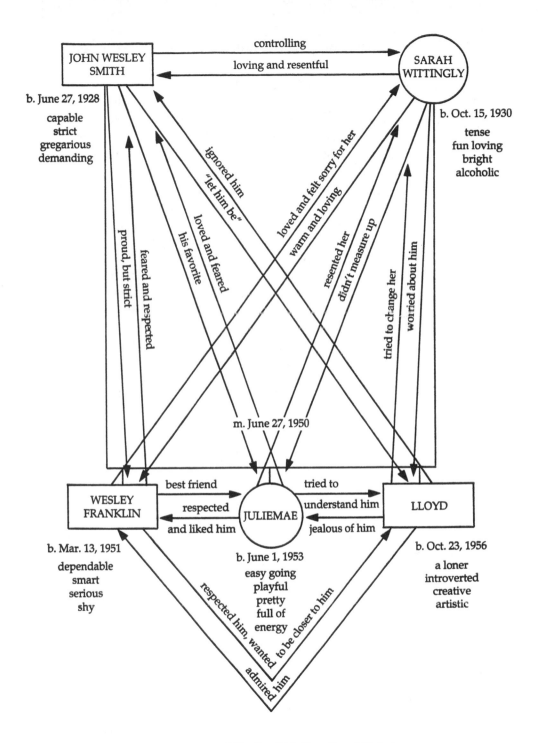

Wesley Franklin Smith's Family of Origin

that describe your parents." I do this because all that you have is your *perception* of your parents and your *perception* of how these core dynamics operated in them. Your perception may fit the reality or it may not. There is a good chance that if your brother or sister were doing this task, he or she would come up with perceptions different from yours. *However, do not let this disturb you.* Your reality of your parents and relatives is your *perception* of them. It was this perception that you responded to when you grew up. It is this perception that is your understanding of them. In fact, if your parents did this task, they may put down adjectives reflecting a perception different from yours! All of our actions are based upon how we see things. There may be a reality out there that is different from our perception, but it is on the basis of our perception that we make decisions and act. Part of maturing is to change our perceptions to fit the reality of life. This is precisely what we are about in this book. We are involved in a process of shifting our perception of our parents and relatives from seeing them as playing a role, such as "mother," to seeing them as the full human beings they are. They were Sally and Mike before they became mother and father.

Since these core dynamics are so central in understanding a person it is advantageous to do the work I am suggesting. The following is an example of how to do this task.

John Wesley Smith

1. Self-Esteem (on a scale of 1 to 10, 10 being the highest)	7
2. A meaning about life, or people, or roles, or any particular event or events that seemed very important.	Life is given to you on a daily basis; therefore live it as fully as possible, enjoy it.
3. An important functional rule and dysfunctional rule.	Functional: "be responsible" dysfunctional: "never make a mistake."
4. Favorite coping strategy when threatened.	Would withdraw, be silent.
5. Quality of relating	Had many social friends and a few close ones; I doubt he ever revealed his deepest feelings to his wife. Related to the children as a parent, even when we were grown.

Sarah Wittingly

1. Self-esteem	4
2. Meaning	It's important to be honored and respected as a person; the father is the head of the family.
3. Rules	Functional: "have fun" dysfunctional: "be a perfect mother."
4. Coping strategy	Withdraw into alcohol.
5. Quality of relating	Emotionally expressive, caring, one or two intimate friends; liked people; feared deep emotional intimacy with husband.

Wesley Franklin Smith

1. Self-Esteem	8
2. Meaning	It is important to be responsible for persons and things and to oneself.
3. Rules	Functional: "pay attention to others" dysfunctional: "always think of others before yourself."
4. Coping strategy	Read books or become superreasonable
5. Quality of relating	Socially friendly, open with trusted friends, sometimes shy.

As you complete this work, be aware of what you are feeling and thinking (besides being tired). Perhaps if you close your eyes and rest easily in your chair, you can more readily be aware of your feelings. Write down your reflections.

After you have rested or feel ready to proceed, place all three genograms in front of you. Just let the genograms speak to you, as it were. Allow any thoughts and feelings to arise within you without forcing any particular line of thought. Just study the genograms and be aware of whatever comes to you. You may then want to write down some of your thoughts or feelings.

I now suggest a more directed line of reflection after you have allowed for the unfocused type of reaction to the genograms. Again I urge you to keep notes of your reactions to these questions.

1. How were your mother and father's personalities and meanings of life developed from their family experiences? What
   did they bring to each other at the time of their marriage?
   As the marriage developed how did their personalities
   and meanings blend and how did their assets and liabilities blend? How did their personalities change due to the
   influence of their spouse?

2. When you came along, how did their personalities affect
   you? How did the way your father and mother related affect
   you? As you grew from a young child into adolescence, how
   did they treat you the same and how differently?

3. What puzzles do you have about these three families or
   members of these families? What questions would you like
   to ask your mother? your father?

4. What do you want from any of these families or individuals
   that you do not have?

5. What do you like and dislike about these families?

As you ponder these questions be aware of how you feel.

Your genograms may be filled with many question marks
beside names and dates. You may know nothing of some of
these people. This is information that you may want to get from
relatives still alive or from whatever records you can obtain.

Your thoughts and feelings, wants and puzzles may provide
you lines of inquiry for family members.

There is another exercise, which some find helpful, called the
Circle of Influence. On a single piece of paper draw a small circle
in the center of the page and put your name in it. Then draw
long and short spokes from that circle. At the end of the spokes
write down the names of all those who influenced you, whether
positively or negatively, from birth to eighteen years of age. Those
who had the greatest influence will be at the end of the short,
thicker spokes and those who had the least influence at the end
of the longer spokes. The circle of influence will contain names
not only of your relatives, but also of teachers, rabbis, ministers,
coaches, neighbors, friends, employers. Often doing this work
awakens old memories, offers new insights about oneself, and fills
out the context of one's impressionable years. Some are deeply
touched by how rich their lives were because of the contribution

of others, while others are surprised by how few people were influential in their early years.

The diagram on pages 104 and 105 is an example of the circle of influence.

Note that to each name you add who they were and how they influenced you positively or negatively. You will also notice in this example that a spoke leads out to Lou Gehrig, the famous New York Yankee ballplayer in the early 1930s. Public figures in sports, entertainment, politics, history, and literature are people who can exercise influence over a young person's life.

After you have done this, write down any feelings and thoughts you are aware of.

The next task, and perhaps more difficult than the genograms, is to make chronologics of the factual events of the maternal and paternal families and the family of origin.

The easiest way to do this is to begin with your own family first. The first date and fact that is entered is the first meeting of your parents that marks the beginning of the relationship that led to the marriage. While they may have known each other since grade school, you enter the event that you think is the beginning of the relationship that explains the eventual marriage. The following is an example of a family of origin chronology.

ROBERT BRONSCOM'S FAMILY OF ORIGIN CHRONOLOGY

1962   John Bronscom, eighteen, invites Sarah James, seventeen, to the junior-senior prom in high school.

1962   September, John enters college; writes to Sarah

1963   Sarah graduates from high school and in the fall enters Kansas State as a freshman; John is a sophomore

1963–66 John and Sarah date constantly, are pledged to each other

1966   John graduates and formerly asks Sarah to be engaged; she accepts

1966   John gets job at Hallmark as card designer

1967   May 29, Sarah graduates, magna cum laude, from Kansas State

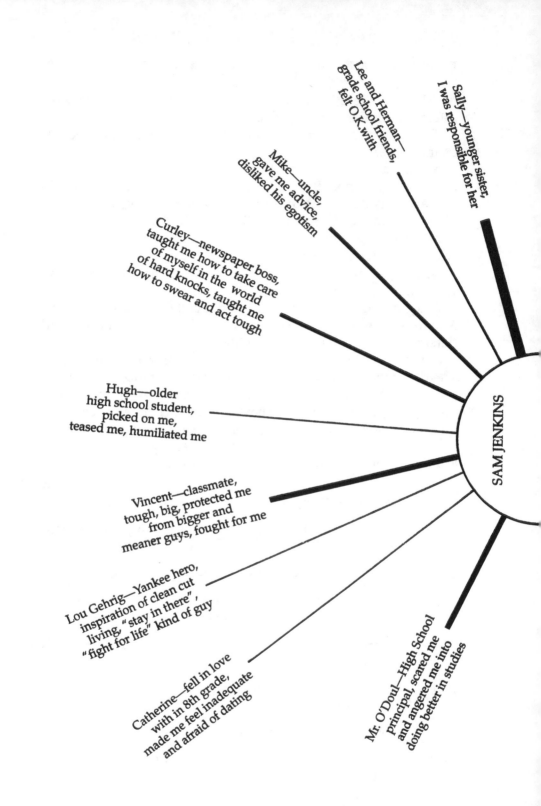

Lee and Herman—
grade school friends,
felt O.K.with

Sally—younger sister,
I was responsible for her

Mike—uncle,
gave me advice,
disliked his egotism

Curley—newspaper boss,
taught me how to take care
of myself in the world
of hard knocks, taught me
how to swear and act tough

Hugh—older
high school student,
picked on me,
teased me, humiliated me

SAM JENKINS

Vincent—classmate,
tough, big, protected me
from bigger and
meaner guys, fought for me

Lou Gehrig—Yankee hero,
inspiration of clean cut
living, "stay in there",
"fight for life" kind of guy

Mr. O'Doul—High School
principal, scared me
and angered me into
doing better in studies

Catherine—fell in love
with in 8th grade,
made me feel inadequate
and afraid of dating

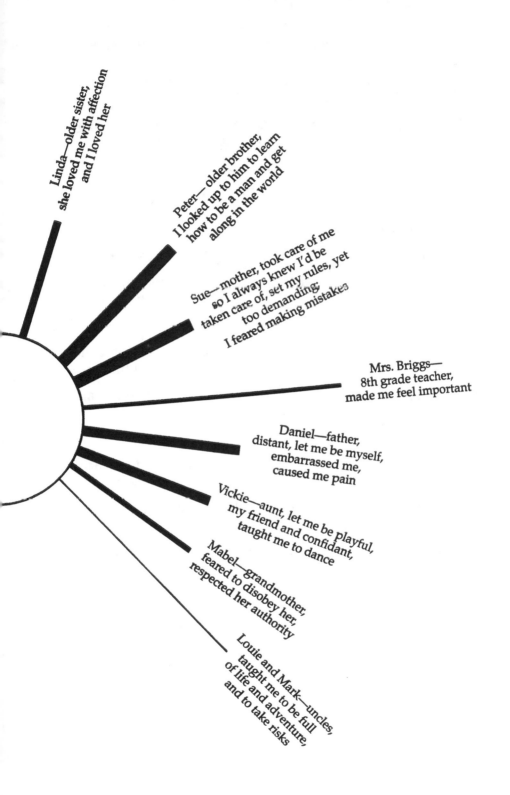

Linda—older sister,
she loved me with affection
and I loved her

Peter—older brother,
I looked up to him to learn
how to be a man and get
along in the world

Sue—mother, took care of me
so I always knew I'd be
taken care of, set my rules, yet
too demanding,
I feared making mistakes

Mrs. Briggs—
8th grade teacher,
made me feel important

Daniel—father,
distant, let me be myself,
embarrassed me,
caused me pain

Vickie—aunt, let me be playful,
my friend and confidant,
taught me to dance

Mabel—grandmother,
feared to disobey her,
respected her authority

Louie and Mark—uncles,
taught me to be full
of life and adventure,
and to take risks

1967	July 22, John and Sarah are married at the First Unitarian Church in Kansas City, Mo.
1967	July, they rent a house in K.C. and Sarah begins teaching English literature at a public high school in K.C.
1968	They become pregnant in January.
1968	October 15, Robert Frost Bronscom is born, the first child of John and Sarah, in Kansas City, Mo., at the Methodist Hospital
1969	John and Sarah become active in the peace movement
1970	John is physically threatened by a neighbor whose son is in Vietnam
1971	September 22, Anna Louise Bronscom is born
1972	Family moves to Palo Alto, Calif.; John works for the Hewlett Packard Company; Sarah tutors part time
1973	Robert falls from the porch and splits open head; twenty-two stitches taken
1974	Robert enters preschool
1975	Robert enters first grade; Sarah resumes full-time teaching
1976	Parents buy first home with three orange trees in front yard
1976	John and Sarah enter marriage counseling for four months; the marriage is helped
1976	Robert becomes a troublemaker at school
1977	Robert does well in school; "falls in love with his teacher"
_____	
_____	
_____	
_____	

The chronology continues, listing all dates and facts that in some way affected Robert's life. The chronology ends with this entry:

1993   January 29, Robert finishes this chronology.

Your chronology may be two to five pages long, listing every event you can think of in your life that you judge had some impact. Besides the examples given above, sickness, deaths, pets, and societal events are all listed, as they have some bearing on the lives of the individuals within the family.

After you do this, rest awhile and just reflect on the work you have done. Be aware of what you are feeling. Then write down your feelings and thoughts.

When you are ready, do the chronologies of your father's family and mother's family. These chronologies should begin at least with the birth date of the oldest grandparent. If you know or can discover some background information on each of them, it is helpful to add that. The following is an example.

PATERNAL CHRONOLOGY — JOHN BRONSCOM'S FAMILY

(John is the father of Robert who is doing this work)

1902   William Bronscom was born February 23 in Omaha, Neb.; he was the fifth child (third son) of seven children (four boys, three girls); his father was a farmer and raised cattle. They were of English descent and had little or no church affiliation.

1904   Thelma Schneider was born May ? in Lincoln, Neb.; she was the firstborn of five or six children; her father was a Lutheran minister in Lincoln; they were of German descent

1930   William and Thelma are married in Omaha in the Lutheran church; they rent a small farmhouse and work for the owner of the farm

1932   Luke Bronscom is born

1934   Mary Bronscom is born

1935   Family move in with William's family on their farm due to the Depression and help with the family farm outside of Omaha

1935 and on. Family visits relatives on all major holidays

1937   Lucille Bronscom is born, third child

1939   Luke enters grade school

1941   Pearl Harbor; Mary enters grade school

1942   William works for defense industry in Omaha; family moves to rent house in Omaha

1943   Thelma pregnant with fourth child

1944   John Bronscom is born; William forty-two years old, Thelma forty

1944   Lucille enters grade school; Mary in third grade, Luke in fifth grade

1945   War ends

1946   William becomes general manager of a Goodyear tire store

1947   Family buys house in nice section of Omaha

1948   Lucille in fourth grade contracts a mysterious illness, eventually diagnosed as a rare cancer

1949   Lucille dies of cancer, twelve years old

1950   John enters kindergarten; Luke is junior in high school, Mary a freshman

1950   John gets a pet, a collie named Sport.

1951   Luke graduates from high school with honors; gets scholarship to college

1951   John enters grade school

1953   Mary graduates and goes to University of Nebraska in Lincoln

1955   Luke graduates from college; gets scholarship to University of Chicago law school

1957   Mary graduates from University of Nebraska; begins working for Dow Chemical as chemist

1958   John, seventh grade, sent to tutoring to raise grades

1959   Sport is hit and killed by a drunken driver

1959   John enters high school; excels in football and baseball, getting Bs and Cs

1962   John invites Sarah to the junior-senior prom

Note that the paternal and maternal families begin with the birth date of the oldest grandparent and end with father and mother's first meeting that leads to the eventual marriage. This event begins the family of origin chronology.

After doing the paternal chronology write down your feelings and thoughts.

The next task is to do the maternal family chronology as you did the paternal chronology.

The maternal and paternal chronologies may seem skimpy compared to your family of origin chronology. This may motivate you to learn much more about the events that occurred in your mother's and father's family while they were growing up. I hope you are so motivated and can get this information. The more you can know, imagine, of fantasize about your mother and father being born, raised, and developed, the more you will see them as human beings like you. It is far more important to have them tell you about *their* childhood than it is to have them tell you about your childhood, as important as that is. Of course, we want to know more about what went on when we were in the early years of our life. However, the way to complete our maturation is to be able to perceive and relate to our parents as human beings, not as parents — which is why it is more important to find out what they went through when they were kids! How did they react, feel? In the illustration of John Bronscom above, how did Robert's father, John, feel during the turmoil between his mother and father that led them to a marriage counselor? How important was it for John to have his pet? How did he feel when Sport was killed? How was it for him to have older siblings so successful in school while he was getting Bs and Cs? How did this make him feel about himself? What enhanced and what damaged his self-esteem? Can Robert identify with any of this? If so, he can begin to shift his perception of John from that of "Dad" to that of "John."

The final task that is so very important is to write a birth fantasy of yourself, your mother, and your father. The fantasy is a fantasy, not a recording of known facts. That is, you take what facts you know and then fantasize the full story of what took place at your birth. I will take myself as an example. At the time I did my first fantasy of my birth in 1975, I knew the following facts. I was born of Bill and Corinne Nerin in Indianapolis at St. Vincent's Hospital, January 26, 1926. At the time I did my fantasy I wasn't sure of the birth dates of my mother and father, so I didn't know for sure how old each was when I came into their lives. I took the four facts — who my parents were, what city I was born in, what hospital I was born in, and the date of my birth — and incorporated those facts into my fantasy. As I remember it the fantasy went like this.

"It was cold that day in Indianapolis. Corinne had been taken to the hospital early in the morning on the January 26 by Bill in the Vealey automobile that Bill had just purchased. This was his first child and he was in his early forties. He was worried for Corinne and for the child. He truly loved and adored Corinne. He knew that she was competent and had had two other children from her first marriage. He had seen what a good and efficient mother she was with Celeste and Nor, but in spite of all this, he still worried. She was in her late thirties and hadn't had a child for eleven years. Would she be all right?

"Corinne worried too, but not as much as Bill. She didn't let Bill know of her worries. She had been praying frequently these last weeks, saying her rosary in French more than once a day. She knew her mother had been praying too. And God would listen to her mother, if He would ever listen to anyone!

"Corinne wanted the baby to be whole and healthy, and a cute baby at that. She wanted to give Bill a very special gift. He had never had a child. Would it be a boy? The Nerin clan would die out if this was not a boy, as Bill was the last living Nerin. He had only one living sibling and that was a sister who never married. So this is it. She didn't think she could have another baby, or at least didn't feel much up to it at her age. She felt confident the baby, boy or girl, would be good looking, as both she and Bill were.

"Bill and Corinne wanted Jo and Harman to be there. Jo was Corinne's closest and favorite sister, and Bill was crazy about her too. And both loved their mutual friend, Harman. So Jo and Harman were there for the big event and to support Bill and Corinne.

"The pains increased in tempo and intensity, and Corinne was taken from her room to the sterile, bright hospital room where all the babies are born. Doc McDevitt was there to deliver. He was more than a doctor; he was a friend of the family.

"They sedated Corinne. The baby came fast. Corinne was out of it and glad it was over. The baby was sound and healthy, and it was a boy! Bill was excited as hell! Jo and Harman cheered. They had brought some champagne and opened it to celebrate.

"When Corinne came to, she too was groggily pleased and smiling. They brought the baby in for the first feeding and Corinne and Bill felt filled with joy. Naturally the name would be Bill, a junior. Corinne had given her gift to Bill, and Bill was grateful to her and to God (he kept his relating to God for special occasions only). Corinne thanked God and renewed her pledge to Him to be the best mother she could be."

Later I called my mother and she verified that indeed Jo and Harman were there! In fact she said that it was amazing how accurate the fantasy was. She countered two pieces of it. The doctor was not Doc McDevitt, and she was really tired and exhausted.

This example shows what a fantasy is. I had only four facts and I made up the rest. I told a story. I imagined what the feelings were, what the thoughts of the people were, what the weather was like, how slow or quick the delivery was, etc.

I strongly encourage you to write a fantasy of your birth, your mother's birth, and your father's birth.

Many people resist doing this. I have found several common reasons why they resist. One is that some people are inhibited in writing stories; they are wedded to facts alone. It is as though only facts count; fantasy is only make believe and therefore of no account. They are the products of the Western scientific mind set. I hope that if this is the way you are, you do not let this stop you from trying your hand at the task. Don't worry about being "right." Since you may have only a few facts, you can't be graded for failing to know or being right.

After you do each fantasy, pause and be aware of your feelings. Write them down after you have tasted them.

This chapter spells out a vast amount of work to be done. Some of you may be intimidated by it. I hope that those of you who do the work will reap many rewards.

I will close by commenting on how to seek information from your relatives without unduly threatening them. Most people who have sought information for the genograms and chronologies have found it to be a most rewarding experience. The parents are pleased that a child of theirs is interested in *their* lives, especially their early years. Such curiosity by a son or daughter honors the parent's life and their families. So, many seeking this information are amazed at how enthusiastic their mothers and fathers are in answering the questions. Many find their parents spending hours talking about their own parents and families. For many, this is the first time their parents have been so open about themselves.

However, in a minority of cases, some parents and relatives seem threatened by such inquiries. Over the years I have learned that there are four common ways parents are threatened. One is that their early lives were painful. So they are afraid of stirring up the memories of that pain. The second way parents are threatened is that they have a strong rule: "Family's business is to be kept within the family." Or they have family secrets. So they are afraid that if they tell their inquiring son or daughter about the family, it will get out. The third way parents can be threatened is that they get the idea that this information seeking is going to reveal them as bad parents in some way. "Why are you interested in this?" they say. Behind that question is the perception that they didn't do a good job and now the son or daughter has to straighten himself or herself out from such a poor rearing. They fear they are being indicted for bad parenting. Sometimes their fear is based on reality because they indeed failed their children as they grew up.

The fourth, and perhaps most subtle threat, comes from the way the son or daughter is seeking the information. Often the person seeking the information has a hidden agenda, which is to change the parent. That is, the person wants some acceptance or approval from the parent and uses the information gathering process in an unconscious way to change the parent. The parent smells this. If the son or daughter is subtly maneuvering the parent to change, it must mean that the son or daughter is not satisfied with the parent. So the parent thinks, almost in a vague and unconscious manner, "What's wrong with me that my child wants me to change?"

When a son or daughter has this unconscious hidden agenda, the parent is threatened and will stonewall the efforts to gain information.

If any of these four reasons are present, there are ways to lessen the threat. Approaching the parent in a nonthreatening manner will encourage the parent to open up. This, of course, will be advantageous for the parent as well as for the one seeking information, for it will bring the parent and son or daughter closer together.

First, the grown son or daughter must examine himself or herself carefully. "Do I have any hidden agendas? Am I still demanding something from my parent that I haven't got? Do I want approval or acceptance?" Another way to look at it is, "Can I truly accept my parents as they are with their assets and liabilities? Can I accept them without demanding any change in them?"

The second part of a nonthreatening approach is to try to assure them that you honestly believe that they did the best they knew how in raising you. It doesn't mean that they didn't hurt you at times or didn't fail you. No parent, including yourself, is perfect. We all fail each other at times. When we do, it is mainly due to ignorance, or being under stress when our faculties are not functioning well, or being frustrated and feeling impotent. So it was with our parents. There is an explanation even for a mean parent, if we dig for it and understand how that parent was raised. So we need to convey to our parents that we truly believe that in their positive and negative functioning they were doing the best they knew how.

Third is to reassure them that you honor the preciousness of their lives and families. You will use the information only in the most confidential way.

Last, we need to approach them with compassion in the sense that we are willing to enter into their pain with them and share it with them. If their childhood was painful, they need to know from us that we are willing to understand and identify with that pain. Thus, they will not bear this pain alone any longer. We will be with them in the pain.

If we have these attitudes, as exemplified to some degree by Jim Ryan, then we will reduce the possible threat that parents may have when we inquire into their backgrounds. Above all, we are interested in this information for our own sakes so we can be more fully embracing and accepting of them as our roots! When they detect that frame of mind in us, they will be open to share their lives and humanity with us. On the basis of our shared humanity we can join them as adults and equals.

Chapter Eighteen

The Amazing Process
of Family Reconstruction

ๆ

UP TO THIS POINT, we have dealt with several ways to reconnect with family roots. These have been through conversing with relatives, remembering past events and data, examining extant records, and using the imagination to fantasize.

But what can we do to reconnect with our roots if there are no living relatives? If we have no knowledge of our parents, as with an adopted person? If our parents and relatives will not enter into these conversations or give information? If our relatives are so enmeshed or overwhelmed in their own feelings that they cannot access their deeper and more subtle feelings and thoughts? (For instance, a father may be so angry that he is not aware of the deeper feeling of loneliness, or a mother may be so hurt by her own parents that she is unaware of her fear to be intimate with her own children.) What can we do if we are afraid or too hurt to enter into dialogue with our parents? If we are too skeptical that any inquiry will bear fruit? If we are too angry to deal directly with a parent or relative? What can be done if we, while knowing much about our roots and able to talk with relatives, still feel puzzled or not healed or not connected in a full human way with parents? What can be done if any of these conditions prevail?

There is an imaginative process through which we can understand our parents and relatives more as human beings than as players of a role in the family. This process was developed by Virginia Satir in the late 1960s. She called the process "family reconstruction." My first book describes in detail this process as well as how to guide a family reconstruction.

Unfortunately the term "family reconstruction" can be misleading. Many people think it is a process to shape up one's current family rather than focusing on the family of origin. Virginia meant the term to refer to seeing one's *family of origin* in a new, reconstructed way, that is, to understand the family one came from in a more adult way. A growing child with his or her undeveloped capacities cannot understand the subtleties, complexities, and depth of the human condition of one's parents and lineage. To understand the full human condition of an adult, one must have developed into adulthood oneself and gone through enough of life experiences to capture these subtleties and complexities.

I have not been able to come up with a more accurate brief term for this process. Perhaps "reconnecting with one's roots," "family roots reconstruction," "redefining family roots" may do it; I don't know. "Parent reconstruction" is inadequate as it suggests the actual changing of one's parents and it limits it to just parents. It is important to understand the humanness of all the significant members of our family roots, which might include grandparents, aunts, and uncles.

How does this process of family reconstruction work?

Family reconstruction takes place within a group of people, usually eight to fifteen in number. The first task is to establish trust and create a safe environment in which to work. The one doing his or her family reconstruction, whom I call the Explorer, having completed the work described in the last chapter, chooses people from the group to play the roles of father, mother, brothers and sisters of one's family of origin; the father's mother and father, brothers, and sisters (the paternal family); and the mother's father and mother, brothers and sisters (the maternal family). In other words, the Explorer picks people to play each person on the three genograms he or she has prepared.

Before I continue I want to say a word about role playing. Playing the roles is very simple. It is the opposite of being an actor or actress. An actress, for example, is told by the director of the play how to play the role. The director has his or her idea of how the players should act and be, and how the scenes should unfold. This is not how to be a role player in a reconstruction. All one has to do is to be herself or himself. As information about the family is given, as the role players are put into sculpted postures, automatically various thoughts and feelings will begin to occur within the minds and emotional systems of the role players. This is hard to believe, but it happens. The more the role player is just naturally herself or himself, the better the job will be done. The more the person tries to figure out how this man or woman was in order to play such a role, the worse the role playing will be. You will see more how this works later on.

To continue, each family, the paternal and maternal families and the family of origin, is reenacted one after the other, the family of origin being the last. The process usually takes about seven hours, which includes an hour or two for building group trust.

Reenacting the family is done by utilizing three processes (in addition to picking the role players), namely, sculpting, portraying scenes (verbally and in pantomime), and fantasizing. I will explain each of these processes and later explain why they work so powerfully and accurately.

Before I go on, let me set your mind at ease. Many people reading about family reconstruction find themselves skeptical about what they read. They are skeptical that family reconstruction works the way the written description says it does. They are skeptical that role players can do what is described. They doubt that a complete stranger can accurately portray feelings, thoughts, actions, and reactions that often actually occurred in the family they are portraying. They wonder how an Explorer who knew little or nothing of a family or member of a family can accurately pick a role player or sculpt such a person. If you find yourself doubtful or skeptical, be at ease. Over the years I have found that this is a common and normal reaction to the spoken or written description of family reconstruction. It is simply very difficult to describe this process in a believable way. Many people need to experience it personally or see it on video tape before they can believe or accept it. To aid you in this I have listed in the appendix how you can secure a video tape showing this process or possibly locate a live family reconstruction to attend.

After the selection of role players, the next step is the enactment of the drama. The first process used is what is called sculpting or body posturing. For example, the Explorer will be asked by the one leading the reconstruction, called the Guide, to place his role-playing father in a physical position that represents how the Explorer perceived his father. So the Explorer may have the role player stand firmly on his feet, legs spread apart, hands on hips, looking straight ahead with a serious look on his face. Or the Explorer may have the role player sit in a chair, slumped over with a drink in one hand and the other arm resting on his lap with a downcast expression on the face.

The Guide may ask the Explorer to position the mother and father of his father (the paternal grandparents) in a sculpture that represents the way the Explorer perceives how they related to each other. Often I will say "John [the Explorer] I want you to put Louis and Marge [the Explorer's paternal grandparents] in a sculpture or physical position that is your picture of how they related to each other before they had kids. Imagine yourself as a famous sculptor. You have two blocks of stone here in these two role players. And you want to form a sculpture of them to be placed in the local art museum so that when viewers see the sculpture they will say 'Ah, this how Louis and Marge related to each other when they were first married.' "

So John, the Explorer, may put a hat on Louis, cock it over his left brow, have him twirl a long key chain in his right hand, and look jauntily at his wife with his left hand in his pocket. John may then place Marge standing on the right side of Louis, with her head tilted back, eyes looking flirtatiously at Louis while standing firmly on her feet with her left hand on her hip.

The Guide then instructs Louis and Marge to remain frozen in that position and be aware of what they begin to feel and think. I keep them in the sculpted position for a minute or two so they have a chance to recognize different layers of feelings and thoughts that emerge.

Relying on information provided by the paternal chronology prepared by the Explorer, the Guide will then tell the role players that shortly after their marriage, they became pregnant. The Guide then places a folded towel or sweater under the shirt or blouse of Marge. The Guide again asks the role players to be aware of what they are now feeling and thinking.

For an experiment, put yourself in the position of Louis (get a hat) and stay there for a minute imagining you are looking at a

Marge posed the way I described. Be aware of any feelings and thoughts that occur to you. Then put yourself in Marge's place, posed as described, imagining you are looking at Louis. Stay there for a minute. Be aware of your feelings and thoughts.

Now to continue the experiment: As Marge, put a folded sweater or small towel under your shirt or blouse to represent your pregnancy with your first child. Place yourself back into the position and see if there are any different feelings and thoughts. If there are, allow those feelings to guide you to move from your sculpted position to a new position that expresses the way you feel. Stay there for a moment or two to see if any other feelings emerge.

Now go back to being Louis, looking at Marge in her new position as pregnant. Be aware of how you feel and think differently. Then allow yourself to move to a new position that fits your new feelings and thoughts.

If you have done this experiment, I think that you will have been aware of initial thoughts and feelings; how a change in the sculpture (the pregnancy represented by the towel) changes the feelings; how moving to a new position affects feelings and thoughts. You can see how in a family system, a dance is created. One sculpture leads to another; one person's change affects the other person. That person's reactive change affects the first, and on it goes.

Just imagine what might happen to Louis and Marge when the baby is born and how they might position themselves in reaction to this new person in their lives. At this point, the Guide may say to Louis and Marge, "Now just let yourself be free to move and express yourselves in words as fit for you."

Marge may lean over and hug the baby, while Louis may be leaning over with one hand supporting Marge. Marge may say, "Look, honey, a baby boy. He's perfect. What shall we name him?"

And Louis may say, "Honey, you did it! I knew you would. He looks just like me!"

Marge: "I think he does too. Shall we name him Louis?"

Louis: "Well I don't know. One Louis in the house is enough; why don't we name him after your father, Edward? Maybe our boy will become a successful lawyer like your dad."

Marge: "Oh, Louis, that would be wonderful — you like my father so much. Come hug Edward; you won't hurt him."

The action and words emerging from the original sculptures comprise the drama, which is the second process. The Guide selects scenes to enact from the paternal family's chronology. Scenes are selected that influence the personality development of the son (who is the future father of the Explorer).

So the Guide may say, "You are pregnant again Marge [putting the folded towel under her blouse], three years after Edward was born. Let's see how the three of you [Louis, Marge, Edward] react to what is happening to Marge." The three will move and speak according to whatever they are thinking and feeling. For example, Edward might say, "Mom, why are you getting so fat?" and Marge would then answer him. Marge and Louis may be inclined to discuss the second pregnancy. As each event from the chronology is announced, the role players are invited to do and say what seems to fit for them. Each one's action stimulates a response in the others, and that response in turn stimulates a new cycle of stimulus-response. Thus the development of the dynamics of the family and the personalities of the individuals within it rapidly takes place.

Let us say that the second pregnancy is another son, named Robert, who will become the father of the Explorer. What are the events that are critical to Robert's development that are reenacted? The births, stillbirths, miscarriages, and deaths of family members are all important. The birth or death of a family member has a critical impact on the family system and stirs up different reactions within the members. How the births and deaths are reacted to influences the personality of Robert. In one sense, "family" may be defined as a system that brings life into the world, nurtures it, and then prepares its members for death, completing a cycle.

There are other events, taken from the prepared chronology, that are also important to enact for the development of the personalities of the members of the family. Such events are moving from town to town, changing schools, sicknesses, taking in a relative, tornadoes, war, fires, robberies. Successes and failures are critical in personality development. How everyone deals with these losses and gains affects the family system and Robert. Examples are Louis losing his job during the Depression, Edward failing in school, Robert's pet dog dying, or, on the other hand, Louis getting promoted and buying a home, Marge saving the neighbor's child from a fire, Robert making the football team, and Edward learning to ride his two-wheeler.

The Guide might then have the role players enact some ordinary family events, which may not even be included in the chronologies but did happen in the family. Such events could be a Christmas or Hanukkah celebration, a birthday, an evening meal, or bringing home report cards. The role players would be told to act on whatever inner feelings they were having at the time.

If the chronology lists any events of any family member getting into trouble, such scenes are important to reenact, such as Edward being expelled from school, Marge getting drunk one night, Robert being suspended from the team, Louis being fired. How the family reacts to these stresses influences Robert. If the chronology has no such events listed, the Guide will manufacture some troubling event. There is not a family in which some trouble has not occurred at some time. It is critical that throughout the reconstruction the Explorer gets a balanced picture of the family. Humorous or playful events must balance the serious ones.

Periodically during the unfolding of these events, the Guide may stop the process to see what the Explorer and the role players are thinking and feeling. Also, the Guide may freeze the action and invite the role players to close their eyes and be aware of which needs are being met and which ones aren't. Then the Guide may invite the role player to move nonverbally to get their needs met in the family. This pantomime is powerful because it forces the role players to act out more dramatically since they can't use their voices and words.

These are examples of some of the events the Guide will be leading the family through. The Guide *never* tells the role players how to act, or what to say, or how to feel or think. That is left completely up to the role players. The role players are sufficiently in the moccasins of the person they are representing to be able to respond appropriately.

The role player is able to identify with the person he or she is playing by means of three processes: the choice of the role player, the original sculpting the Explorer does, and the ensuing drama.

Choosing the role players is important. Why did the Explorer pick this one person from among the fifteen in the group to play Louis? Why not pick some other person? There is something in that particular person that strikes the Explorer as fitting the character of Louis more than any of the other fourteen.

Why did the Explorer sculpt Louis in the precise way he or she did, posturing his feet, legs, body, arms, hands, fingers, facial expression, direction of eyes? The Explorer could have made a thousand different sculptures. Why this one? Because that particular sculpture, more than any other, resembles Louis in the Explorer's unconscious mind. The Explorer cannot tell you fully why he or she settles on this one sculpture above all the other possible ones. The choice of the role player and sculpted posture is explained more by the unconscious information the Explorer has than what he or she is aware of.

The unconscious knowledge of the Explorer is activated when the Explorer picks the person and sculpts that person to be Louis. This is sufficient to initiate the role player into the feelings and thoughts of the person he or she is playing. As each event in the life of that person and family occurs, the role player responds on the basis of the original set of feelings and thoughts stimulated by the first sculpture. Of course the original set of feelings are enlarged and developed as the various scenes unfold and information is given to the role players about their backgrounds and life.

This is why the role player is left free to react in any way he or she feels, rather than having the Guide dictate the way the person should feel or think or act.

After the role players are sufficiently into their roles, the Guide can resort to fantasy to complete the story of the family. Let us go back to Louis, Marge, Edward, and Robert. After the family has played out some events up to, say Robert's tenth year of life, and the Guide judges that Robert is fairly well into the role, the Guide may say the following:

"Now I want the four of you to close your eyes and just take in what I'm going to read to you from this chronology. You will have your own spontaneous reactions to what you hear. Allow your fantasies to come alive in response to what you hear.

"1960 — When Robert is eleven and Edward is fourteen, Edward, a good athlete, is hit in the forehead by a baseball and is unconscious for five days in the hospital. He finally recovers, but his mental functioning is permanently impaired. From being an 'A' student he now requires special education.

"1964 — Robert, age fourteen, becomes class president of his high school freshman class.

"1964 — Robert refuses to go out for high school athletics, even though he is a gifted athlete; he joins the drama club instead.

"1965 — Edward is passed through high school and gets a job as a carpenter's assistant.

"1966 — Robert gets Bs and Cs and is continually reprimanded by Louis and Marge who know he is capable of straight As.

"1968 — Robert, eighteen, graduates from high school and refuses to go to college; he takes a job in a factory and continues his drama activities in the local amateur theater.

"1970 — Robert, twenty, meets Mary while trying out for a new play; they begin dating and fall in love.

"1972 — Robert and Mary get married; Edward is the best man.

"Now, the four of you open your eyes and report to the Explorer what your fantasies, feelings, and thoughts have been as you have heard these facts from the chronology."

Louis, Marge, Edward, and Robert each relate their reactions to what they have heard.

For example, Robert says, "After Edward's accident, I felt so bad that I didn't think I deserved to be better than my brother, so I kept myself back. I didn't want to outshine him, make him feel bad. That's why I didn't go out for the high school teams. I also held back scholastically. I did enjoy drama but there was something missing for me. I only felt half alive. Then I met Mary. She accepted me as I am. I became glued to her; she became my entire life. I could take my mind off Edward."

This illustrates the use of fantasy in family reconstruction.

As the life of Robert develops, from birth to the meeting of Mary and marrying her, the Explorer, John, has now come to understand some aspects about his father that he never knew before. John begins to see why his father, Robert, was so attached to and later dependent upon his mother, Mary. As a youngster, Robert felt he should never outstrip his stricken brother, Edward, so that Edward would not feel bad (this is the meaning Robert put on this event). As Robert grew, his parents could not figure out why he slipped so badly in school and refused to participate in athletics. Robert felt stung by this lack of understanding on the part of his parents. In fact, his parents only pressured him to do better. So Robert didn't feel accepted by them either. Feeling only half alive, Robert's self-esteem was severely damaged.

Then Mary enters his life and she, while not understanding the significance of Robert's background and the meaning Robert made of Edward's accident, nevertheless accepted him as he was. She was involved in theater activities as he was. That was a common bond. Also, Mary detected the sensitivity of Robert, and she was attracted to that. She also perceived his care for the underdog, and this was another attraction. Furthermore, as Mary showed her acceptance, appreciation, and attraction for Robert, he became more and more enamored of her. He desperately needed to be accepted and appreciated.

As John, the Explorer, sees all this for the first time, he understands many things that had puzzled him about his father. Most of all, John sees the vulnerable human being that Robert is and begins to relate to Robert with this new perception. He perceives him more as a human equal to him than as a father superior to him. Family reconstruction has made it possible for John to have this new way of connecting to his father. He can now accept him as another human being, not just in the *role* he played in his life as his father. Even if Robert could have talked to his father about his childhood, his father might have been unaware of these unconscious life decisions he had made over the injury of his brother. So he could not have explained them to his son.

The above is an illustration of the process of family reconstruction and the benefit it can have for one who does his or her reconstruction. Note that the ultimate benefit for the Explorer in seeing mother, father, and others as human beings is *that this allows the Explorer to accept these roots as part of self.* If we see our parents fundamentally as mother and father, it may be difficult to accept them as part of themselves. Often there have been some rough moments and hard feelings between adult child and parent. But if mother and father are seen to be as human as ourselves, it becomes much easier to accept them as part of ourselves. So in the process of accepting them as belonging to us, we are making ourselves whole. We are integrating ourselves with our roots. It is from this sense of wholeness, this acceptance rather than nonacceptance, that all the other benefits such as increased power, confidence, self-esteem, and self-identity flow.

I have described in this example only the development of the father's family. Regardless of whether or not the Guide starts with the paternal family, the reenactment would be followed by the development of the other families, in this case the maternal family and family of origin. Thus all three families, the maternal and paternal families and the family of origin, are enacted. By far the *most important families to reenact are the paternal and maternal families*. It is in these families that the Explorer sees the development of father and mother from birth to marriage. When we come into the world we meet our parents as grown adults and begin to know and form our perceptions of them from that point on. Thus we see them as big and experience ourselves as small; we see them as powerful and experience ourselves as weak; we see them as all-knowing and experience ourselves as seeking knowledge; we see them as competent and perfect and experience ourselves as prone to failures and mistakes. By going back to the maternal and paternal families we now see and experience our parents also as small, weak, dependent, needy, ignorant, and fallible. This is a profound shift in the way we perceive them. It enables us to *experience* them as equal to us, human as we are. We would not have this experience if we reenacted only the family of origin.

From this illustration you can see how role players in a family reconstruction can reveal aspects about a mother or father that perhaps the real parents could not. In the case of Robert, he might not be aware of why he became so dependent on Mary, which led him to fear alienating her and to over-rely on her for his self-esteem. Perhaps Robert would even deny that he was too dependent on her.

This example also shows us how family reconstruction can help heal wounds between the Explorer, John, and his father. For instance, let's say that when John grew up, his mother was overly demanding and domineering. When John would turn to his father for support in fighting for independence against his mother, his father never supported him. Robert, because of his fear of alienating Mary, always backed Mary, even at those times when he felt John needed support. So over the years, John developed a hidden resentment toward his father and grew distant from him. He felt that he had to find himself without any support from his father.

Now what does this enactment of family members do for John? Having done his reconstruction, John can now understand the deeper dynamics of his father's struggle for his own self-esteem, the meaning he made out of Edward's tragedy, the rule he had never to hurt anyone, how he coped with all this by withdrawing from studies and athletics, and how this affected his relating to Mary, his hidden savior. Now John can understand why Robert feared contradicting Mary and never supported him against his mother. John can even identify with some of those feelings of low self-esteem and the struggle to maintain it. John's resentment toward Robert fades, his compassion grows, and he can now become closer to him, closing the distance that has existed over the years.

So family reconstruction is a powerful, and relatively quick, process whereby we can gain a new and more balanced perception of our parents, grandparents, aunts, and uncles as well as heal old wounds and scars left over from childhood.

I will conclude this chapter by sharing a few letters I have received from those whose reconstructions I have guided. And I will give a remarkable account of the accuracy of a family reconstruction done by a team of students learning how to do this process with an Explorer.

The following are excerpts from a letter written to me by an Explorer four months after his family reconstruction. "Something has been churning inside and I couldn't quite put a label on it for the whole time. I have a friend who reminds me regularly that change is slow, painful, and undramatic. I guess I have to say *that* is what has been churning inside me. Subconsciously, I may have been preparing myself to unlearn a lifetime pattern of self-defeating behaviors. Anyway, although I didn't recognize it as such at the time, I gave up smoking in November. I still have cravings, but I do not want to do something so injurious to myself any longer. About a month after I gave up smoking, I started getting really aggravated with myself about procrastination. I'd have to say that is my most self-defeating behavior of all. I put things off until they either don't get done or they get done sloppily. It was a tormenting habit which I just couldn't seem to break. It had become such a sick behavior that I would put off doing things I knew I would enjoy just because I had committed to do them. It is all tied to resentments. Mostly, resentments against my parents. I didn't think I had any left, but I did. Silly and childish, but that's how I'd felt all these years. Like a child faking maturity. I had a pretty good idea what the mature behavior was supposed to look like, and I managed to take it pretty well most of the time. Still, I felt like a child inside, and I am still about fourteen in some ways. Humility forces me to admit that.

"I'll have to say, I am gradually seeing improvement. I am doing more and more things without the kinds of delays I used to use. It doesn't feel like such a drain or chore. I don't feel the kind of childish resentments about having to do the dishes or make the bed that I used to. I am beginning to *want* to do things because it feels good. It's hard to believe I'm forty-two years old and still dealing with such silliness. It's also hard to believe I have allowed it to have the negative impact it has. I ain't fixed yet, but I am working better. I am convinced that I wouldn't be at this place in my growth without the family reconstruction. That gave me a very important key. Learning that I have held myself back in order not to 'hurt' my brother was a big surprise. I believe it is a pivotal issue...." (It is coincidental that this actual letter expresses the same dynamic of fearing to hurt his brother as we saw earlier in the fictional account of Edward.)

This letter expresses the changes occurring in this person's life four months after he did his reconstruction. He does not give an explanation of how the reconstruction worked within him to influence these changes other than the reference to his brother. All he says is that his growth was helped by the reconstruction. This is another example of how becoming appropriately rooted, as with Jim Ryan, releases energies for today's needs. It adds to one's strength, self-esteem, and maturity. His "going home again" helped him mature.

About a month later I received a second letter from this Explorer. In this letter he expresses in a wonderfully symbolic way the deeper dynamics at work in seeing one's parents as human. This letter is important also because so many today are wrestling with addictions of one sort or another.

"I haven't told you, but it seems fitting and perhaps helpful to you if I tell you now. I'm alcoholic. I was in my seventh month of recovery when we did my reconstruction. It's been about a year now. I believe the reconstruction was very helpful. I'd recommend it to anyone. In fact, I believe it would be very useful to anyone in a recovery program. Especially, I believe people in recovery programs would benefit from a reconstruction before doing a fourth and fifth step. That's where we search our past and unload all the hurts we've had or inflicted on others. I'm not trying to rewrite the program, but it does seem that those of us who combine outside therapy with our AA programs do get healthier a little more quickly than those who don't. I believe FR could be a big help....

"My FR set me free of many resentments I hadn't gotten down to in my fourth and fifth steps. As I was more able to accept my parents and their human frailty, I was able to accept their mistakes. In that, I found my own faults less horrid. What was a gradual change seems to be gaining momentum, rather like a balloon rising when it has been loosed from a mooring. The difference is, I have to work to get the progress, but it isn't as difficult. It doesn't feel like I'm working against the odds now. It feels as though I am going in a positive direction and I don't have to go back where I was. Always before, I lived with this burdensome sense that some unseen force was going to retract me back into the state I had struggled to get out of. That sense was real. It happened over and over. I don't have that sense today. I know I can go back, but I don't have to. Always before, I felt powerless. I always had that sense that no matter how hard I worked at it, I was just going to slide back down again sooner or later. Today, I know I have a choice."

When he saw his parents as human with their own frailties, he could then "accept their mistakes." In accepting their mistakes he was accepting them as part of himself. And in doing that he is *accepting himself!* Thus, he was able to say, "I found by own faults less horrid."

Note this significant statement: "Always before, I lived with this burdensome sense that some unseen force was going to retract me back into the state I had struggled to get out of. That sense was real. ... Always before, I felt powerless." What is this "unseen force"? I think it is the power of his parents who taught him a set of meanings, rules, and coping strategies that he learned so deeply when he was so vulnerable as a child. When he *experienced* his parents as human equal to him in the reconstruction, the godlike hold that this set of learnings had over him was released. The power of his godlike parents was reduced in size. His connection now to his parents was not that of child to parent, but that of adult to adult. The powerlessness of the child is now replaced by the power of an adult, *which he became when he gained the new perception of his parents as human, equal to him.*

The next excerpts are from a letter of an Explorer who had a very troubled and confusing family background. She suffered the trauma of incest. She was very confused about the facts of her genograms and chronologies. They were filled with question marks indicating that she was guessing at most of the data. Once she left home at an early age, she maintained little contact with her family. She was angry at them, afraid of them, and hurt by them. Nevertheless she was preoccupied with her family roots, almost to the point of obsession. She seemed very emotional, yet I detected in her a remarkable resilience. She asked to do her reconstruction. I consented. I could see not only her resilience but how she was stuck in her growth and that sorting out her family would be of great help to her. So without much assured accurate information we proceeded. It was a wonderful experience for her. It motivated and gave her courage to go back to her home state to make contact with those remaining of her extended family. Here is some of what she wrote to me.

"I just came back from meeting my aunts and grandmother. My family reconstruction process keeps on. I feel fortunate that I was welcomed. I learned a lot about my families. Both sides had dysfunctionality. I learned that my father had died.... I'm still sorting out who did what to whom. I've had a lot of different feelings about going down there and meeting everyone who is left. Some anger for what I may have missed, some satisfaction at learning about the house in my memories, some sadness for what wasn't and will never be, and questions. What am I hoping to find with all this searching and exploring? Is it worth it? Is family so important that we will disrupt our lives to go in search of this unknown? I've been processing these questions since my return and I am coming to some conclusions. As much as I have tried to be this person that didn't really need anyone or anything, I realize I have failed miserably in this endeavor. No matter how hard I have tried to be an island unto myself, I haven't been able to pull it off. *What I have found from my search is a sense of belonging.* No matter what these families are like, no matter what they have done to me and no matter how little contact I have had, have now, or will have in the future, I belong to them. And because I can say and feel that I belong to them and to all that is behind me I can now see that I belong to myself, and what I do from here on out is up to me. It is up to me what I do with what

I have received from these families, these multitudes of people that it took for me to be here writing this letter. They all stand behind me and somehow that seems so awesome and I feel so complete because I know this now. Yes, it is worth it. Family is that important. I am so grateful to you for my family reconstruction; I have no words to convey how important this has been for me."

Three months later I received another letter from her. Again I quote a few excerpts.

"Tonight my brother called me. This is the first time he has done this in twenty-two years. I've written him requesting communication from him, but nothing seemed to be coming from it. To this day he has no idea of the sadness I have felt from this lack. We mostly discussed his kids and business; however, we briefly made some contact about the secrets that have kept us from being able to reach out to each other. . . . He told me that he is still overwhelmed by the information and he feels that we will talk about it eventually, just right now it is still hard for him. . . . Anyway the present of himself was very meaningful for me. It also reinforces my realization that most of what I have blamed myself for has had nothing to do with me — it has had to do with where people were at that time. The best I can do is leave the door open and go on with my own life. I still feel sad that there are so many others who do not get to make peace with themselves, let alone with others in their family of origin."

These quotations reveal how the family reconstruction enabled the Explorer to reconnect with her family, how beneficial that was to her, how that enabled her to feel "complete." They also reveal how all this has allowed her to lessen her resentments, to understand that each person is dealing with life from within the parameters of his or her unique makeup and experiences, and to take responsibility for herself and life.

Note the implication in the statement, "And because I can say and feel that I belong to them [her family] and to all that is behind me I can now see that *I belong to myself, and what I do from here on is out is up to me*" (emphasis is mine). It is in accepting one's roots that one accepts oneself. Belonging to one's family is belonging to self. This is turn allows one to be responsible for oneself. How many there are who are not able to take responsibility for their own actions and lives. They either blame others or feel helpless. My hunch is that they have not achieved an *appropriate* connection to their roots!

I talked to a young man in his middle thirties who had done his family reconstruction five months ago. He told me that he had just returned from spending five days with his parents for the first time since his reconstruction. While in their home, he became quickly aware of how much calmer he was compared to previous visits. He was aware of how much of his anger had dissolved, though at times he did get angry at them during the visit. He saw them in a "softer way." As he saw them he kept having flashbacks to his family reconstruction, which helped him stay connected to his new understanding of them as his peers.

He then went on to say that the reconstruction helped him make significant changes in his daily life. "What changes?" I asked. His answer was a mild surprise to me. I thought he might say things that I had heard before, such as, "I'm closer to my wife and kids," or "I've lost weight," or "I've quit smoking," or "I've changed jobs." Instead he said, "It was powerful to have my genograms aired in public and to have the group respond to them. It *made my family real*. Before my family was like—unreal. I knew I existed! Somehow my family looks like a family; I have a reverent sense of being in a family. It took away an existential feeling I've had all my life, like "I don't belong here, I don't have a place. . . . Now I feel I do belong and I do have a place!"

This was the significant change he noticed in his daily life. This is a far deeper change than losing weight or changing jobs. His statements express a remarkable increase in basic self-worth — "I do belong; I do have a place." It was the statement of a man firmly rooted.

These three are examples of family reconstruction at its best. Not all reconstructions bear such wonderful fruit. I suspect that out of the eight hundred or more reconstructions that I have guided, there have been some five or six about which I have wondered if much value was gained by the Explorer. The value received is different for each person of course. For some the value is tremendous, for others less so. I can only speculate why these five or six seemed to bear such little fruit. I have had the experience of guiding one person through two or three family reconstructions. In these cases it is most obvious that the person achieved different results in each reconstruction. In each case the Explorer was at a different stage in her or his growth, which explained the different outcomes. Perhaps these five or six were not ready for much movement or that I was really off target in my guiding.

Often those who have heard about family reconstruction but have not experienced it first hand wonder if the drama that unfolds and the attitudes of family members that are expressed are really accurate or purely fictional. It has been my experience that 80 to 90 percent of what is portrayed is true-to-life. When Explorers take the information gained in the family reconstruction to their parents or aunts and uncles, they find that much of it is verified.

I want to relate a case in point and then consider what happens if the information revealed in the reconstruction is not accurate.

Several years ago a woman did her reconstruction under the guidance of three of our students who were learning how to guide family reconstructions. We usually videotape the reconstructions we do in our groups to give to the Explorer. Later, the Explorer can look at it to relive the experience as well as see aspects that might have been unnoticed during the reconstruction itself.

This woman, whom I shall call Marie, showed the videotape to her sixty-five-year-old mother and sister. She wrote me a letter about this experience. I quote a section from this letter.

"This last July my sister and mother visited me in my home. I must say that it was with great trepidation that I invited them to view the video of the reconstruction with me. I wondered how it would impact them. Together we watched the crude video of my reconstruction. It was hardly a professional tape! At times we looked at someone's back or the floor and struggled with the portions that were inaudible. But we watched it all, hour upon hour until three in the morning. At the conclusion the table before us was heaped with soggy tissues as we wept our way together through the experience.

"You will remember that the woman, Velma, who played the role of my mother reported that despite having participated in a least twenty reconstructions, she had never been anyone who experienced as much pain and fear as my mother. In fact, she went home that evening and had a asthma attack. That is exactly what my mother has done her whole life — somatized her pain. . . .

"My mother's first tearful reactions were that the whole reconstruction was extremely 'accurate and very revealing.' In a letter, later, she says 'how overwhelmed my father must have been (he had been raised in an orphanage)...the torture he lived through about what he had done.' She wished longingly that the reconciliation scene had happened in real life. 'I really think I could watch it several times and each time there would be a new revelation,' she writes."

In this case the information provided was verified by Marie's mother.

But let us consider the case where the information and attitudes expressed by the role players are not accurate.

There are two considerations here. First is the case where the Explorer's parents are alive and willing to talk about the results of the reconstruction. In correcting the facts and attitudes, the parents or grandparents explain their own feelings and attitudes. This reveals them as more fully human to the Explorer than before the family reconstruction was done. In reaction to the experience of the role players in the reconstruction the parents tell the Explorer what really did happen as they grew up, whereas prior to that they had not disclosed such feeling and thoughts. Often the experience of the role player triggers the memory of the real parent into revealing experiences that the parent would not have remembered if not stimulated by what the role player said.

The second consideration is when the Explorer has no access to the relatives to verify the reactions of the role players in the reconstruction. What then? The Explorer does not know for certain if these happenings and attitudes are correct or not. *But that is not the most crucial point.* What is crucial is that these people, who later become mother and father of the Explorer, are seen as vulnerable human beings. In 98 percent of the cases, the Explorer senses that what is revealed makes sense to him or her. If it does not make sense, it offers a scenario that the Explorer can react to in order to fantasize a human situation that does make sense! And in the very process of making up a scenario that does make sense, the Explorer, in his or her fantasy, is seeing a parent as a human being. That is the point.

What is important to me is to see my mother and father as human. Thus, I can accept them as equal to me, which means I "grow up to their height," as it were. It doesn't make any difference whether the way I see them as human squares with reality or not. A profound shift has occurred within me. I perceive and emotionally feel different about them. I shift from perceiving them as parents over me to perceiving them as humans equal to me. One thing we know for sure; they are human just like me, having the same core dynamics I have described earlier, the drive to be loved and to feel good about themselves, the drive to make sense out of life, to follow their interior rules to be good and accepted by their parents, to cope to survive when threatened, to have satisfying relationships with significant people, to find intimacy in life. The details of how these basic dynamics are played out in life differ from person to person; the dynamics are the same. Indeed, Mom and Pop are Mary and Robert.

Chapter Nineteen

Why Family Reconstruction Works

❧

WHY IS IT that people who do their family reconstruction find that what unfolds before their eyes makes so much sense to them? Why is it that when some of the facts and basic attitudes displayed by the role players are checked out by the Explorer, they are found to be true to a large extent? In other words, how can the role players portray so authentically the people they are chosen to play?

People are often amazed at the accurate choices of role players that an Explorer makes. I have guided reconstructions in many different settings. While the most common setting is within ongoing groups of 8 to 15 people wherein each person does her or his reconstruction on a monthly basis, I often guide family reconstructions in large groups of 40 to 150 people where someone volunteers to be the Explorer. In this latter situation the marvel of choosing extremely appropriate role players is most dramatic because the Explorer has never met the person he or she chooses to play the role of his or her mother, father, or grandparents. Often role players make comments at the end of the family reconstruction such as, "It's funny you picked me; I too came from a Scandinavian background and I lost my mother at the age of six as you lost yours at seven," or "Did you know that I was raised in Iowa just ten miles from where your grandparents lived? In fact, our family knew some of those people?" or "I'm amazed; I too have an identical twin just like your father. How did you know to pick me?"

Are these merely coincidences? I don't know. Perhaps that is all there is to it. However, this kind of thing happens quite often.

But more impressive and dramatic is what happens nearly 95 percent of the time, namely, that the Explorer picks role players who become so thoroughly involved in their roles that over and over the Explorer will make comments such as, "My mother would say the same thing you are saying," "You even move your hands like my uncle," "You're so much like my grandmother, I can't believe it!" The Explorer, after hearing and seeing a scene unfold or after witnessing the life of the mother and father develop, will say such things as, "That really fits," "That makes sense," "That's my mother!"

The Explorer is able to identify with the basic feelings, thoughts, reactions, and attitudes of the role players as apt representations of what the Explorer knows of the actual family members. It is this "fit" that makes the reconstruction so believable to the Explorer, so when the parts of the reconstruction unfold that the Explorer knows nothing about, it all makes sense. Puzzles vanish, mysteries are solved, the members of the family are more thoroughly understood.

Examples of such mysteries are:

- why Mother abandoned the kids,
- why Dad committed suicide,
- why Uncle Mike took to drink,
- why I could never get close to my younger brother,
- why Mother was put in an orphanage as a child,
- why Father left home so early,
- why Grandmother and Grandfather slept in separate rooms,
- why my older brother was so driven to be successful,
- why Aunt May never married,
- why was I adopted?
- did Mother really not like me?

- did Father want a boy instead of me?

- why was Mother so depressed?

- why was Father so angry?

What is even more astonishing is that in the majority of cases the Explorer finds that what is presented in the reconstruction occurred in actual fact, especially the basic feelings and attitudes. I refer you to the example at the end of chapter 18.

Is this a coincidence? I believe not. Then what explains how the Explorer can so aptly pick from a hundred strangers that one person who can so accurately portray the family member he or she is picked to play?

I think that two factors partially explain this phenomenon. One is that each of us has an enormous amount of information stored in our unconscious about members of our family. Second, each of us has a tremendous capacity to "read" another person intuitively. Since both of these factors operate unconsciously, we obviously are not aware of how much information we do have about our family and we are unaware of how great is our ability to detect what a person is like.

Neurobiological research tells us that the brain records the myriad impressions that are taken in by our bodies through the skin or sense of touch as well as through the senses of hearing, smelling, and seeing. This process begins in the fetus before birth. We are becoming more aware of the influence a mother's diet, her intake of drugs, alcohol, and nicotine, and her emotional state can have on the fetus in her womb. These factors mostly affect our unconscious.

We also know that our chromosomes, genes, and DNA contain some sort of a mosaic of people and influences from the past.

A simple illustration of how much information we take in unconsciously is the kind of dreams we have concerning a practical detail. For example, I dream that I am on a motor trip and I am involved in an accident. I awake realizing that indeed I am going to take a trip and I must drive to the airport. I look over my car before I leave and notice that my left rear tire is almost flat. What has happened is that my eyes took in this impression the day before, but I paid no conscious attention to it. In my dream, my unconscious brought my attention to this practical detail. You may have had dreams like this yourself. This does not imply, of course, that all dreams are of such a practical nature.

So over the years, beginning in the womb at the joining of sperm and egg, we have been taking in all sorts of information, including that of our family. We have been taking in consciously and unconsciously how our parents feel about each other, about themselves, and about us. We have been assimilating in the unconscious mind facts, details, events, and stories about our family roots. While we cannot recall much from before the age of three, four, or five, the information is there. If we deem it important, we can access much of it.

Over the last thirty years, modern research and experimentation have confirmed how much information we do have within us. I will relate here the work of one of these researchers, Stanislav Grof, M.D. He is a psychiatrist who has spent over thirty years researching nonordinary states of consciousness, beginning in his native land of Czechoslovakia in 1957 with experiments with LSD. He migrated to the United States and was chief of psychiatric research at the Maryland Psychiatric Research Center and assistant professor of psychiatry at Johns Hopkins University School of Medicine. He later developed a breathing process that he calls holotropic breathing, which effectively accesses the unconscious.

He reports that many of his subjects, when in an nonordinary state of consciousness, were able to recall memories from the first days and weeks of their lives with almost photographic accuracy. More astonishing he says, "Subjects can relive elements of their biological birth in all its complexity, and sometimes with astonishing objectively verifiable details. I have been able to confirm the accuracy of many such reports when the conditions were favorable; this frequently involved individuals who previously had had no knowledge of the circumstances of their birth. They have been able to recognize specificities and anomalies of their fetal position, detailed mechanics of labor, the nature of obstetric interventions, and the particulars of postnatal care. The experience of a breech position, placenta previa, the umbilical cord twisted around the neck, castor oil applied during the birth process, the use of forceps, various manual maneuvers, different kinds of anesthesia, and specific resuscitation procedures are just a few examples of the phenomena observed in the perinatal psychedelic experience" (*Beyond the Brain* [Ithaca, N.Y.: SUNY Press, 1985], 39).

His subjects were also able to recall "ancestral experiences, elements of the collective and racial unconscious in the Jungian sense, and 'past incarnation memories' frequently ... related to specific historical events and costumes, architecture, weapons, art, or religious practices of the cultures involved. LSD subjects who relived phylogenetic memories or experienced consciousness of contemporary animal forms not only found them unusually authentic and convincing, but also acquired extraordinary insights concerning animal psychology, ethology, specific habits, complex reproductive cycles, and courtship dances of various species" (ibid., 42).

This research indicates how phenomenal is our store of knowledge. Yet, we are for the most part unaware of it. It is, I believe, from this vast storehouse of knowledge residing in the unconscious that an Explorer draws from when he or she is picking role players.

The apt choice of a role player also depends on the capacity of the Explorer to detect the kind of person a role player is. How is that able to be done?

Scary as it may seem, our bodies record and manifest in many ways our life's history and our ancestral roots. In a sense, we are open books, no matter how hard we try to put on a "poker face." Luckily perhaps, the ordinary person in an ordinary state of consciousness cannot read this open book. So most of the time we can remain private and hide our true selves from others. But an extraordinary person, such as the fictional keen observer Sherlock Holmes or a clairvoyant or an ordinary person in an nonordinary state of consciousness, can read the open book of another human being.

Again, modern science offers us evidence that our body does contain our past. It seems that every thought a person has creates an emotional and physical response; every emotion a person feels creates a mental and physical reaction; every physical stimulation creates a mental and emotional response. More and more scientists now think that there is no separation between mind and body. The mind and the body are one and the same. The mind is the body and the body is the mind. *If this is so, then any experience that we have takes on a physical component and is part of our bodily makeup.* Our personal history of human experience is recorded in our bodies. Ernest Rossi, Ph.D., writes: "Where is the connection between mind and body? Can you see it under a microscope? Can you measure it in a test tube?

"It was really a struggle that required a lot of dogged determination to plough through the new medical and psychophysiological texts that were buzzing about mind-body relationships, stress, psychoneuroimmunology, neuroendocrinology, molecular genetics, and neurobiology of memory and learning. These fields all deal with concepts and data that most of us have not even heard of if we have been out of school for more than ten years.

"What was most irritating in my investigations was the realization that none of the specialists who seemed to know something ever shared their knowledge with those outside their narrow area of expertise. As I put the facts and implications of the different specialty areas together, I kept coming up with what seemed to be bizarre notions that apparently were based on solid research but no one seemed willing to acknowledge.

"For example: Is there really a mind-gene connection? Does mind move not only our emotions and blood pressure, but also the very genes and molecules that are generated within the microscopic cells of our body? Is there any real evidence for this? Well, if you push any endocrinologist hard enough, he/she will admit that, 'Yes, it is really true!' Under mental stress, the limbic-hypothalamic system in the brain converts the neural messages of mind into the neuralhormonal 'messenger molecules' of the body. These, in turn, can direct the endocrine system to produce steroid hormones that can reach into the nucleus of different cells of the body to modulate the expression of genes. These genes then direct the cells to produce the various molecules that will regulate metabolism, growth, activity level, sexuality, and immune response in sickness and health. There really is a mind-gene connection! Mind ultimately does modulate the creation and expression of the molecules of life!" (*The Psychobiology of Mind-Body Healing* [New York: W. W. Norton, 1986], xiii–xiv).

Another piece of evidence that the mind changes the body is the remarkable results of the placebo effect. The placebo is a preparation containing no medicine, but is administered by a physician, for example, who tells the patient that it is a certain drug that will produce certain effects. The placebo has no chemical capacities to produce the predicted results. However, people who take the placebo, *merely by thinking* that this is a medicine that will work, do actually produce a chemical change in their bodies and effect a cure! For example, there have been some thirty double-blind studies demonstrating that Valium is no more effective than a placebo in treating anxiety.

How many times have you looked at a stranger, say in the supermarket, and said, "That's an angry person," "That person is depressed," "That man has no energy," "That's a sad lady," "That's a happy person." How did you come to think that? You probably read the body of the person. The person is a stranger, but the body has tight jaws and "angry eyes," or the body may be slumped over and moving slowly, or the face may have "sad eyes," or the body may be moving with a spring and a smile on the face.

The important meanings we have made out of life's events are recorded in our body. The rules we have taken on for life, the ways we cope with stress, how we relate or don't relate to others are marked in the body.

I will cite some examples. A study was done at the University of Chicago as reported in *The Creation of Health* by Norman Shealy, M.D. The researchers studied two hundred executives at Illinois Bell Telephone. About half of the subjects had physical stress symptoms as a result of changes in their lives, whereas the other half had very little. The hundred who had few stress symptoms were found to view change as an opportunity for growth; the others viewed change as a threat to their security.

So the meaning one attaches to life affects what happens in the body. Dr. Shealy further reports, "Even individuals who smoke, overeat and practice other unhealthy habits have a decreased risk of illness if they have a strong support system. There is indeed considerable evidence that 'love is more important than healthy living.' In my own study of one hundred retired nuns, sixty-eighty were over the age of eighty and about eighteen were over the age of ninety. All but one of them seemed to be in reasonably good health and she was one hundred. These individuals tended to be over-weight, under-exercised, and to have a high affinity for caffeine, chocolate and sugar. However, they were extremely content with their lifestyle and obviously outliving many outside the convent" (*The Creation of Health* [Walpole, N.H.: Stillpoint Press, 1988], 344).

This is another powerful indication of how the meaning a

person finds in life is recorded in the body. An overweight, chocolate-loving nun has a body with a fine immune system.

The above research gives evidence of two important facets of our personalities; one is that we have recorded within us, mainly on the unconscious level, vast sums of information about our lives, families, and backgrounds, and the other is that our body is a reflection of our lives because everything that happens to us affects our physical makeup.

So in a family reconstruction, an Explorer can tap into the unconscious storehouse of information about his or her family and history. Furthermore, an Explorer can detect from another person's body and actions what that person is like in terms of attitudes, feelings, and life history. The way that information is tapped into is most often *not* overtly conscious. That is, the Explorer doesn't look at a person and think, "Ah, that person's father comes from Sweden and was the firstborn in the family, like my father, so I'll pick him." The information is tapped into in an unconscious way. It's like, "I don't know why I want you to play my father, but something in me tells me you're the one."

Often in guiding a family reconstruction, when the Explorer is picking role players, I will make comments like, "Trust your guts," "Let your stomach pick the person," "Let the person you want latch onto you," "Don't try to be correct," "Don't figure it out, just feel good about the choice." All these statements help the Explorer access his or her unconscious.

Another most important element needed to access the unconscious, besides being in an altered state of consciousness, is to *believe* that all that information is stored in the unconscious and to *believe* that one can get to it. Let me illustrate this phenomenon by discussing dreams. Often people tell me that they never dream. But brain research shows that every human being dreams. Most often we dream in our light sleep prior to awakening. Some people, due to childhood nightmares, don't want to "dream," i.e., remember dreams.

When I can convince people who "never dream" that their dreams are their friends, that they *do* in fact dream, and that they can remember their dreams if they want to, often these people begin to remember their dreams for the first time in their lives. Some get so good at it that they remember a dream almost every night and even keep dream journals. For them to remember their dreams, they had to *believe* that they do dream and *can remember* their dreams and they had to *want* to recall them.

In summary, an Explorer can make such apt choices of role players because (1) the Explorer has information about the family of origin and ancestry hidden in the unconscious, (2) the Explorer can and believes he or she can access that information, and (3) when in an altered or nonordinary state of consciousness, the Explorer can access that information from the unconscious.

The most remarkable illustration of all this is the case of adults who were adopted as infants and "know" little or nothing about their biological parents. It is amazing how the adopted persons can do the reconstruction even though they think that they have no information. The case of adopted persons is so important that I treat it separately in the next chapter.

It is this unconscious information that is utilized to a great extent when an Explorer does sculpting. Most often I ask the Explorer to make the various sculpted postures of individuals and family constellations nonverbally. Working nonverbally in the art form of sculpting is another way of being in an altered state of consciousness. Artistic expressions such as music, poetry, painting, and sculpting are expressions as well as stimulants of the unconscious, perhaps more than the conscious.

So in both role choosing and in sculpting, Explorers are going beyond what they consciously know and are making available new information about their parents and members of their family roots.

Now the question rises, granted that the Explorer is choosing role players and sculpting them based on information consciously and unconsciously known about the Explorer's family, how can the role players be so well fit for their roles? No matter what our differences are as people, whether we are old or young, rich or poor, educated or not, black or white, Indian or Oriental, city-bred or country-bred, single child or one of many children — all of us share the same basic human nature. We think, imagine, feel, dream. We want to be loved, understood, respected. We want to feel good about ourselves. We have all felt anger, disappointment, grief, joy, excitement, fear. We all have a mother and father. We all had an umbilical cord.

Because we share a common human nature, there is a way that one person's basic feelings, manner of making meaning, attitudes, coping with threat, and striving to feel good about oneself can be experienced by another. Sometimes I am asked, can an American really play the roles of a Chinese, Indian, or African? In my experience with guiding family reconstructions, I have had no problems in guiding a Chinese, Japanese, French, German, or East Indian person's reconstruction when the role players were Caucasian Americans. While a person's culture has meanings and rules that may differ from those of a white, middle-class American, the American understands what it is like to make sense out of things and to live by rules. And when that person hears of the family background, is sculpted, and acts in the constellation of family events, that person becomes in a sense Chinese or Indian.

The experience, of course is not identical to the exact experience of the real person whose role is being played, but it is shared in an analogous fashion. For example, each twin of identical twins raised in the same family has his or her unique human experience. The twins understand each other analogously.

Another factor explaining how the role player can play the role so authentically is the oneness of body and mind. This means that when my body is sculpted a certain way it tends to stimulate a certain set of feelings, desires, and thoughts.

For example, if I am sculpted with my feet firmly planted, my right arm, hand, and index finger rigidly pointing to another, my left hand on my hip, and a scowl on my face, I will begin to feel anger, power, and tightness in my body. If I stay in that position for several minutes, I will begin to feel isolated. I may have thoughts of disdain or hate. If I am sculpted kneeling on my right knee with my hand on my heart, looking up at a standing person with a pleading look on my face, I will begin to feel weak, shaky, helpless, depressed, with thoughts of "I'm sorry, it's my fault, I'll do anything you want." If kept there long enough, I may begin to feel a growing rage.

Just as every thought and emotion has a physical response in the body, so when the body is shaped a certain way it will feel a certain set of feelings.

In summary, sculpting is a powerful means to access the unconscious and it is a powerful tool to engage a role player because of our common human nature and the oneness of mind and body. Sculpting combined with apt choice of a role player can produce an authentic portrayal by a person of the mother or father or grandparent of an Explorer. After the basic set of feelings and thoughts are stimulated, then the scenes that unfold in dramatic form offer the Explorer a powerful understanding of the deeper nature of his or her mother and father — especially within the maternal and paternal families.

There is another factor explaining why family reconstruction works so well. It is in the use of role players rather than the actual family members. In other words, you may ask, if the actual family members were present during a reconstruction, why should they not play themselves?

The reason role payers are used rather than actual family members is a subtle one. Parents tend to be protective of their children, even those who are now fully adult. As a result, they may not want to reveal their negative thoughts and feelings, nor the painful events in their own maternal or paternal families.

Also parents are often bound by their own internal rules of life, such as, "don't reveal family secrets," "what you don't know won't hurt you," and the incest rule. These rules inhibit parents from being frank about negative, painful, and sexual elements of their personal lives. Role players are not so inhibited.

But there are two even more important reasons why role players are of greater advantage than the real family members. First is that each family member has her or his perceptions of the family history and of the persons in the family that differs in some ways from the Explorer's perception. Therefore, family members could attempt to maneuver the reconstruction to fit their perceptions. In the midst of the reconstruction, this could be irritating to the Explorer, who needs to be free to move at her or his own pace from an old perception to a new one. Also the Explorer has no familial emotional connection to the role player and knows that the role player, in contrast to the actual family member, has no vested interest in the outcome. This allows the Explorer to be more open to accepting a new perception.

Secondly, family members are enmeshed in feelings in a way that does not allow them to be aware of the more delicate feelings lying beneath the more dominant feelings. It is these delicate feelings that reveal how truly human they are. A role player can more easily be aware of these delicate feelings.

For example, take the father whose self-identity is wrapped up in being the financial provider for the family. His self-esteem rests upon his ability to be successful in business and to provide for his wife and children. So he works long hours and becomes single-minded about business affairs. Feeling good about being the husband and father he should be, it is possible that he is unaware of a certain loneliness lurking within him. He is unaware of needing affection from family and wife. The real father may not be in touch with that and therefore not able to reveal it in a family reconstruction. A role player could be in touch with that missing part. When the role player can reveal that, the Explorer can get a more tender appreciation of his or her father.

Another reason why family reconstruction works so powerfully is that it uses live people in live scenes, providing a three-dimensional quality to one's knowledge. Family reconstruction touches one's eyes, ears, and body; it involves all of one's senses, not just the intellect. Therefore it is most suited to produce a holistic effect, i.e., a bodily, emotional, mental, and spiritual effect.

There are some other elements that influence how effective family reconstruction will be. The principal one is the degree of motivation that the Explorer has in discovering new pictures of her or his family root members. The greater the motivation the less defensive will the Explorer be in gaining a perceptual shift regarding his or her mother and father. The greater the motivation, the more thorough will be the preparation for the reconstruction, i.e, the genograms, chronologies, and birth fantasies. Some highly motivated Explorers talk to practically all the accessible living relatives, gathering facts and information about the early history of the family.

Another important element is the degree of trust the Explorer has in the group and Guide or Co-guides. Family reconstruction can be scary to many people. That fear is reduced when the Explorer trusts the skill and caring of the Guides and the confidentiality of the group.

Over the years I have come to appreciate another factor that powerfully influences the quality of a reconstruction, that is, the degree of love among the people in the group. I am referring to an ongoing group meeting monthly for one day over a period of ten to twelve months in which each person does his or her reconstruction. Some groups seem to have members who grow in their love and caring for each other more than in other groups.

I don't know the reason for this, but it just happens. When the love is so great that you can feel it, the reconstructions are very rewarding not only to the Explorer but to all the members of the group. The group experience, once a month, itself becomes a catalyst for love to grow and for members to be more sensitive and understanding, more accepting of others as they are. The group experience helps develop the members' capacity to love. The family reconstruction group can become a growing vortex of love. When this happens, I for one, experience it as spiritual experience.

In a sense the group becomes a surrogate functional family. There is an openness in sharing appreciations, irritations (such as being late to the group meetings), questions, and wants or desires for oneself. This surrogate functional family counteracts the experience of the dysfunctional family some of the group members may have come from. This adds another reason for seeing one's relatives as human: "If they were not so restricted in their families, they would have been nurturing." Family reconstruction often shows how one's parents were inhibited from manifesting the deeper human instincts by their own rearing, rules, and learnings. Family reconstruction can show how the family could have been if the parents were free to be loving, understanding, and accepting. Being in a functional group underscores this reality.

Another reason why family reconstruction is effective is illustrated by the research of James W. Pennebaker of the Department of Psychology at Southern Methodist University. He has studied individuals who have had traumatic experiences. His investigations reveal that when they confront and talk about their traumatic experiences, psychological and physiological benefits result. On the other hand when persons with traumatic experiences conceal or do not talk about them, they have increased disease rates as well as emotional difficulties.

Part of Pennebaker's research involves subjects writing personal accounts of their traumatic experiences (reported in "Confession, Inhibition and Disease," *Advances in Experimental Social Psychology* 22 [1989]). Two results of this research bear upon the process of family reconstruction. Keep in mind that in family reconstruction traumatic experiences are often revealed or reenacted. Examples are the death of a parent when a child is still very young, a divorce or abandonment, an alcoholic parent, a severe illness, the accidental death of a sibling, a near-fatal accident, and physical or sexual abuse. Also in many reconstructions traumatic events are disclosed to others for the first time by an Explorer. Or the Explorer may remember an event that has been lost in amnesia, leading the Explorer to confront this experience for the first time.

What is fascinating about Pennebaker's research is that when subjects wrote about these traumatic experiences for the first time, after years of keeping the events secret, their handwriting changed! Some would switch from cursive writing to block lettering, some had pen pressures or slanting of letters different from when they were not writing about the traumatic experience. This indicates that the subjects moved into an altered state of consciousness when they dealt with the previously undisclosed traumatic experience. This reinforces my point about people being in an altered state of consciousness when they do their reconstructions.

Pennebaker thinks that when a person breaks out of a rule that inhibits a certain behavior, in this case the rule to keep secret the experience, that puts the person in an altered state of consciousness. This coincides with the experience of so many Explorers who are breaking the rule of "keeping family secrets," or "don't show your dirty linen in public," or "our business is nobody else's business." The mere breaking of such family rules is enough to put the Explorer in a nonordinary state of consciousness.

The second result of this research that bears upon family reconstruction is the result of simply writing down accounts of one's traumatic experiences. Contrary to common thought, dredging up unpleasant experiences *did not* have negative results in the individuals. It produced highly beneficial results.

Pennebaker's experimental subjects (college students) were asked to write about their traumatic experiences and their feelings about these events on four consecutive days for twenty minutes each day. The control group did not write down their feelings and facts concerning traumatic experiences. The researchers found that these experimental subjects felt upset and had increased blood pressure immediately following the writing. However, the subjects visited the Student Health Center for illness significantly less in a six-month period following the four days of writing than those students in the control group.

Furthermore the researchers found that these experimental subjects' blood samples showed *improved immune function*. Those who disclosed their traumatic experiences in the writing for the first time exhibited greater immune improvement than those who had disclosed their traumatic experiences previously. No wonder they had less illness in the months following the disclosures.

Now if individuals can have such beneficial results from simply writing about a traumatic event and their feelings about it in four consecutive days for twenty minutes in an anonymous environment, what greater results could happen to a person doing her or his family reconstruction? The person spends hours researching the material prior to the reconstruction itself; the family reconstruction offers the person a most real and lively experience using role players; the person is disclosing one's family of origin and maternal and paternal families with whatever painful experiences occurred in those families, not anonymously, but to a group of trusted people; the individual is doing this in a group that offers support to the person. I think the Pennebaker research provides evidence that suggests how beneficial family reconstruction can be for those willing to enter into the process. As far as I know, no one has tested the immune systems of Explorers before and after their family reconstructions. Perhaps some day such a study will be done.

In conclusion, family reconstruction works because:

- Explorers have a huge amount of information about their family roots within their unconscious

- this unconscious information is accessed when picking role players

- due to the mind-body unity, Explorers are able to detect the kind of persons the role players are that fits the unconscious (as well as conscious) knowledge the Explorers have of the family members

- the use of sculpting accesses this unconscious information as well

- due to the mind-body unity, sculpting easily generates feelings and thoughts appropriate to the relative the role player is enacting

- role players are much more effective than actual family members in a family reconstruction

- family reconstruction offers a three-dimensional presentation appealing to the body, senses, and intellect. Other forms of reconnecting to family roots (except that of conversing with family members) offer mainly an intellectual approach.

Family reconstruction works best when —

- the Explorer is highly motivated

- the Explorer trusts the guide and members of the group

- there is a high degree of love in the group

- traumatic events are openly faced and dealt with.

Chapter Twenty

Family Reconstruction
of the Adopted Person

❧

AS I HAVE SAID EARLIER the family reconstruction of an adopted person demonstrates most clearly the value of connecting with and accepting family roots as part of oneself. It also demonstrates most sharply how much unconscious information we have within us. When I guide the reconstruction of an adopted person, I guide the Explorer through the biological family of origin and maternal and paternal families. The adopted person may think that she or he knows nothing about the biological parents, but as the reconstruction develops it is amazing how the adopted person acts as though she or he knows much about the family background.

First of all, many such individuals want to do the genograms and choose role players of the adopted parents and their maternal and paternal families instead of the biological families. However, I insist that it is far more important to enact the families of the biological parents. So far my insistence has paid off. This may be due to the kind of person who is interested in doing a family reconstruction.

I urge the adoptee to do the biological parents because these are the real parents and roots of the adopted person. Furthermore, I have found that many adopted men and women have some special issues that they deal with all their lives. I suspect that whether these issues are present within a person depends on a variety of factors, such as their age when adopted and how the adopted parents treat the reality of the biological parents.

The first issue is a feeling of "not belonging." For some, not all, it takes on the additional sting of feeling rejected. The wrenching away from the biological mother is a primal loss. This primal deprivation of one's roots gives the sense of not belonging and can easily lead the adopted person to interpret this as a basic rejection. This is in spite of the fact that, in most cases, the biological parents are not rejecting as much as providing for the child because they determine that they cannot adequately care for the child. As a result, many adopted individuals seem to be very sensitive to anything that looks like rejection. Having been so hurt in an almost primal way, and in spite of all the love of the adopted parents, many adopted persons still are wary of being rejected and are afraid of being alone. For example, they can easily interpret someone looking away from them as "they don't like me," whereas another person would not even pay attention.

The second issue I have found in many adopted persons is that there is a deep, almost unconscious feeling of not being normal. It is more like a feeling that something is "strange with me." I think it comes from the adopted person's being perceived as "belonging" to the adopted family while suppressing the feeling of not belonging biologically. I had not noticed this phenomenon until I began doing family reconstructions of adopted individuals. At the end of the family reconstruction I often hear the Explorer say something to the effect, "Well, I guess I'm normal after all." That is, in experiencing in the reconstruction his or her birth taking place in a hospital with the mother having labor pains and struggling to deliver, seeing the momentary happiness of knowing it is a sound baby, seeing the pain of realizing that this baby will not be kept — all this tells the adopted Explorer in the pit of his or her stomach, "I came into this world just like everyone else! I do belong biologically — even though my belonging was short lived!"

There are other adoptees who do not have this experience of "not being normal." For them it is just an awareness of being different. This is not always perceived as negative. In fact, it can be a positive perception in that one's uniqueness is honored so that it is okay to be different from others.

The third issue that some adoptees have to deal with is a feeling that "I'm bad" or "My parents are bad," which of course can redound to "I'm bad." That is, "If my parents had to give me up for adoption, there must be something wrong with them and/or me. After all, I am their seed." Of course, this feeling can be felt by those who are raised by biological parents who neglect or abuse their children.

The fourth issue I have found in many adopted people is a strong need to discover one's identity. This, of course, is true for many people who want to do their family reconstructions or trace more thoroughly their roots. Discovering more deeply "who I am" takes on a greater edge for those who don't even know their biological parents. "Where I am from" tells me much about who I am. Adopted persons need to know about their biological parents and ancestry to get a fix on who they are, what they are, and how they fit into the scheme of things. It is the chromosomes of the biological mother and father that the adopted individual has, not those of the adopted parents. Knowing I have brown eyes like my biological mother somehow makes me feel more complete.

So in a family reconstruction when the Explorer sees the biological parents, often with their families supporting and counseling them, struggle with the decision to keep or give up the baby, and then decide to give the baby up, the Explorer most often realizes in an emotional way that he or she was not rejected. At least the Explorer sees that his or her characterological faults were not the reason for the adoption. Most adopted individuals know this intellectually, but the early emotional interpretation of being given away as rejection is still strongly lodged within the adult adopted person. The three-dimensional family reconstruction with real people playing these roles has a powerful emotional impact on the Explorer, counteracting the effect of the earlier emotional feeling of rejection.

Counteracting the feelings of not belonging, of being strange or negatively different, of being bad, of having to find one's identity are reasons for insisting on doing the biological parents and their maternal and paternal families in the reconstruction.

As I said earlier, it is in doing the family reconstruction of an adopted person that the power to access the vast amount of information in the unconscious is dramatically revealed. The Explorer is encouraged to overcome the syndrome of "I don't know my biological family, so how can I pick role players?" After the initial hesitation the Explorer begins to get into the spirit of the reconstruction, picking role players, making up names for them, trying to figure out dates of births, and so on. They carefully think through such questions as, "Did your mother have any brothers and sisters? Where was your mother in the birth order of her family? How old do you think your father and mother were when they conceived you?" It is amazing how the Explorer will pause, perhaps fingers to lips, pondering, and then blurt out, "They were seventeen and eighteen," or "My mother was the last of six and my father the middle of five," or "My mother's name is Jane, my father's is Chris; her parents are Thelma and George and his parents are, let's see, Max and Susan." All this is done so thoughtfully and slowly, as if the Explorer is reaching down deep within to pull out these answers.

Then when the Explorer is asked to sculpt, for instance, the family that his or her mother grew up in, it is amazing to see how long it can take, the amount of care invested, the many changes the Explorer makes as the sculpture unfolds, the utterances from the Explorer while doing the sculpture, such as, "No that doesn't look right," "That's it!" "No, turn your face slightly down," "Not so much pressure with the hand on the shoulder," etc.

I ask myself, where does all this come from? Why is the Explorer making the sculpture this way and not in a thousand other ways it could be done? Why the insistence of these small adjustments? Why doesn't this on that "look right"? What is the Explorer comparing this sculpture to?

The only answer I can come up with is that the Explorer is accessing some information buried within the unconscious and/or in his or her genetic inheritance.

As the family reconstruction unfolds, you can see the Explorer nodding her or his head in agreement with what is taking place. It begins to add up, to make sense. Often during the family reconstruction, the Explorer will recall an anecdote or a piece of information about the biological family that she or he had completely forgotten.

At the end of the reconstructions of adopted persons most often there is a satisfying sense of realness, relief, and often joy. There is also a certain sadness in not knowing these parents in the flesh. The impact on the Explorer in doing the biological families is tremendous. It goes a long way in redressing the sense of not belonging and of feeling strange or bad. It gives the Explorer a greater sense of self-identity.

I recall a case in point. A man in his late thirties wanted to do his family reconstruction. He had been adopted at birth. He knew little about his biological parents except that they had lived somewhere in Arkansas, where he was adopted. He had a strong feeling that his parents were teenagers when he was born.

He made up the genograms completely out of his imagination, those of his biological parents and the families of his mother and father. He chose members of the group to play all these people. He was slow and deliberate in the choosing, looking at each person carefully. He spent a great deal of time and attention in forming the sculptures. It took about four hours to develop the biological maternal and paternal families and the family of origin. Great attention was given to the birth scene and drama concerning whether to give the baby up for adoption or not.

One of the interesting things about this reconstruction is that the woman he chose to play his mother was someone he had never met before. This reconstruction was done in a one-day workshop, not in an ongoing group. After the reconstruction was finished, this woman told the group that she had had difficulties in keeping the babies that she had conceived! She had had several miscarriages and one tubal pregnancy.

So this person, who had not been kept by his own mother, picked from a group of some twenty-five people the one woman who had not been able to keep children of her own. What an apt role player! Was this a coincidence? Or was it due to the explanations offered in the last chapter?

At the conclusion of the day the Explorer told the group how grateful he was for this experience. It was very moving to him. (This we knew as he cried several times during the reconstruction.) He said it was rich and genuine enough, on some level, for him to want to search for his real parents.

Two months later he told a friend that he could stop blaming and that he was quitting his job to move to the state where he thought his father might be. He had been doing some investigations since his reconstruction and was very anxious to discover his parents.

The family reconstruction of an adopted person does indeed

reveal dramatically how much information we have within ourselves that we are not aware of and how we can make that information available to ourselves. It validates one of the principal reasons family reconstruction works as it does. It reveals how crucial it is to be connected in an appropriate way with our roots.

Chapter Twenty-One

Preparing Your Grown Child to Be Your Equal; Retiring from Parenthood

ஒ

IN THIS BOOK I have dealt with the need of adults to perceive and accept parents, as well as other members of one's family roots, in a new way rather than to perceive them in the roles they played in our lives. The thesis has been that adults must see their relatives primarily on an equal level as human beings and as friends, if that is possible. The focus has been on how parents can be seen differently, i.e., as Jane and Howard.

In this chapter I want to change the focus from one's parents to one's sons and daughters. If it is critical for adults to reach full maturity by perceiving their parents as human, it is also critical that adults who are parents see their own sons and daughters as human. That is, grown sons and daughters need to be seen not primarily as sons and daughters but as adults equal to parents.

If parents are dedicated to helping their children grow into full maturity, what can they do? That is the subject of this chapter.

When parents help their grown children to become equal to them, they are performing the final act of parenting. They are assisting their offspring to reach that final stage in personality development. It is the final act of parental love, ushering in a new, more expanded way to love — as friends and equals.

When this shift takes place, the parents are also doing themselves a favor. They are finalizing their job of parenting, They are retiring from a job that has preoccupied them for twenty to thirty years. Several stories will illustrate these two aspects.

Over the years I have heard parents, usually after they have taken the journey to meet their own parents as human, say, "What can I do to help my children eventually see me as human?" or "I'm going to collect data, pictures, and memorabilia for my children so that they will know their family history," "I'm going to start a journal of my thoughts and feelings so my kids can see what went on in me when they were young."

In addition to helping adult children see us as their equals, we need to deal with retiring from parenthood. This was recently expressed by a forty-nine-year-old man, Doug, who pleaded with me, "Bill, tell me, how can I get my kids to deal with me just as an adult and not as their father. They are in their twenties, and I swear, at times, they act like they are fourteen years old. They get spiteful, angry, hurtful. At other times they are too damn dependent. I'm tired of being their father. It's time they stand on their own two feet."

This father has a somewhat unusual situation, though it is becoming more common these days. He is divorced. His former wife, the mother of his children, still wants to be a mother and keeps the grown children dependent on her. While he wants to be released from the role of parenting, he is not as influential as the mother over the children's behavior. Secondly, I suspect, the grown children might still be angry at Doug for failing to deliver some fathering either before or after the divorce.

Be that as it may, Doug's plea — how can I stop being a parent? — is a plea of many parents.

I fear that there are far too many parents who unconsciously cling to their parenting roles long after their children have left home. They may even complain about how their children depend too much on them, but beneath that complaint is the overriding need to feel wanted and needed as a parent. It is by remaining the "good parent" that such parents find their self-esteem and value. Their self-esteem seems to rest on that alone.

This is unfortunate. It means that such parents have no other sources for their self-esteem, and this is understandable. After spending the major portion of our time and psychic energy for some twenty to thirty years in being a parent, it is hard to relinquish what we have been doing.

I think that the first thing parents must do to help their children perceive them as equals and to relinquish the task of parenting is to face themselves honestly. Do I really want to stop being a parent? Do I want to end the satisfaction I get from being needed and wanted this way? Do I really want my kids not to lean on me? Do I want to let them be as they are and let go of trying to get them to behave as I want them to? Is my self-esteem, my good feeling about myself, too bound up with how good, decent, and successful my kids are? Am I too shattered if one or more of my kids fail — fail personally, fail as parents themselves, fail in their marriage. While feeling upset, sad, or disappointed, and while offering all the support I can, can I still maintain my bearing in spite of what the kids do when they are beyond their teens? If so, then I can let go of trying to control their lives, marriages, children, and outcomes.

Another way to honestly face ourselves is to ask ourselves a set of questions on the other side of the coin. Do I really want my kids to see me in any light other than as their parents? Do I want them to see me in my full humanity, i.e., do I want them to see my weaknesses and failures as well as my strengths and successes? For their sakes, when they were young, I presented myself as strong, knowledgeable, competent, and in charge. Now as they grow older do I want them to see my weak, negative, fearful side?

Am I willing to tell them of the fearful events of my life as I grew up, as I was first dating, as I was engaged, and as I experienced the early years of my marriage and parenting? Am I willing to tell them the troubles I had with my parents? How willing am I to disclose to them acts and situations that I am ashamed of if I think this would be helpful? Am I willing to confess to them the times and ways I failed in my early and middle years? Am I willing to relate how I coped with my emerging sexual powers? Am I willing to tell them what made me feel sad, what my losses were as I grew up? Can I tell them of my broken dreams and unfulfilled wishes? Can I tell them of my positive and negative thoughts about their birth and growing up?

If I am afraid that my son or daughter cannot take the negative, embarrassing side of me, then am I not still regarding them as children rather than as strong adults, as strong as I am?

The positive side must not be neglected either, however. Can I tell them of the excitement and dreams I had when I first met my future spouse? Can I tell them of the joys of my childhood, how I regarded my parents, what I loved about them? Can I tell them of the special moments in my life? Can I tell them of my spiritual experiences? Can I tell them what I've learned from my life's experiences that I deem valuable?

So in order to help sons and daughters see their parents as equals, the first thing parents must do is to face themselves. They must address the question, do I want to stop being a parent and let the growing children see me as human? If parents really do, then they have made the most important step in this direction, the final step in being a good parent. This is the step that helps the grown child achieve full maturity. When this happens, the son or daughter feels grown-up inside, no longer in the one-down relationship to the parents. The daughter or son has now moved up to an equal level with the retired parent. It is no longer Mom and Dad; it is now Helen and Doug. I think there should be a ritual symbolizing this double shift, namely, parents perceiving their offspring as equal to them and the grown children seeing their parents as equal to them.

All this may seem obvious. But I don't think it is, and furthermore I do not think there has been enough emphasis on it historically, culturally, and in the field of developmental psychology. Perhaps the greatest proof of this is our own English language. Has it ever occurred to you that there is no word in the English language that symbolizes the meaning of an adult child or of the biological parent who is no longer parenting? And as far as I have been able to find out, there are no such words in any language! In his book *They Have a Word for It* (Los Angeles: Jeremy Tarcher, 1988), Howard Rheingold lists words in other languages that have no equivalent in the English language. I could find no such words in his book.

I have had to resort to terms like "adult child," "adult son," "adult daughter," "grown child." I have had to repeat descriptive statements every time I wanted to talk about the "parent who no longer parents," "the parent who now relates on an equal adult-to-adult basis with her or his adult child," the adult child "who now perceives the parent as a friend rather than as a parent." How much simpler it would be if there were a word meaning that.

Today's literature is loaded with "adult child" labels, for example, "the adult child of alcoholics," "the adult children of divorced parents," "adult children of sexual abuse." The problem with this terminology is that the word "child" must still be used. The very expression "adult child" connotes the child-parent relationship, not an adult-to-adult relationship.

It is the same with the word "parent." Even if it is used in a sentence with the meaning of coequality with an adult child, it too connotes parenthood. It is as if once a parent, always a parent. Of course one is always a parent in the sense of being the one who participated in the conception of a child. But a parent is not always a parent in the second meaning of "parent," which is to be the one who rears the child. That task eventually ends. There is no word that symbolizes a man and woman who are finished with the job of parenting.

So let's make up our own words based on Latin and Anglo-Saxon roots. The word for the grown son who now perceives mother and father as human beings equal to him is "parsu"; the word for the adult daughter is "parlia." The word for the father who no longer parents is "viramecus"; and the word for such a mother is "winameca." To put it into a diagram:

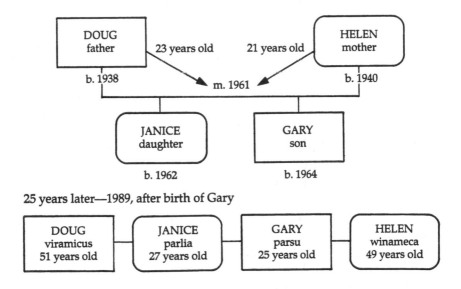

25 years later—1989, after birth of Gary

An account of a camping trip would go like this. "Janice, the parlia, and Gary, the parsu, were companions on a camping trip to the Cascades with Doug, the viramecus, and Helen, the winameca. The four had a great time sharing chores and telling stories about their intimate lives. Doug told many stories about his viramecus, Thomas Edward...."

When we have to use words like "adult child" and constantly refer to Doug and Helen as father and mother or parent, we continually reinforce the connotation of the child-parent relationship. We need terms that connote and reinforce the adult-to-adult relationship. Now I doubt that "viramecus," "winameca," "parlia," and "parsu" will become common currency in our language. However, I wonder if the day will come when we will invent adequate labels for this reality. It might be a sign that we have recognized the significance of this step of development in our culture and in our understanding of developmental psychology.

Psychology is beginning to take note of the need to see our parents as human and as a result to have an adult-to-adult relationship with them. In 1981, Don Williamson, Ph.D., wrote in the *Journal of Marital and Family Therapy:* "The existing literature on the family life cycle has been surveyed recently. There has been no recognition of what this writer believes to be a crucial family stage or task.... This task is to terminate the hierarchical boundary between the adults or young parents, and the older parents, now the grandparents." What he means here is that the adult child-parent relationship must change to an adult-to-adult peer relationship. He continues, "Perhaps the field has been slow to recognize this stage or task and slow to face the naked power issue head on" (October 1981).

Perhaps the idea is gaining some ground. Today it is more common for grown children to address their parents by their first names than by "Mother" and "Father."

Parents who desire to help their children relate to them as persons based on their shared humanity rather than on the parenting task can do many things to achieve this goal. As I said, the first step is to really decide to do it.

The next important ongoing task is to introduce your child to your weaknesses and failures. As the child develops from childhood into adolescence and then into young adulthood, the child begins to shift from seeing Mom or Dad as all-powerful and all-knowing to seeing them as vulnerable and fallible.

I have had many memorable counseling sessions with parents disturbed with their acting-out teenagers. In front of the teenager I ask the father and mother if they had ever lied as teenagers or gotten into trouble. If so, I ask them to describe the incident to the teenager. Often the very trouble the teenager is in is the exact trouble the parent got into when the same age as the teenager. The revelation of the parent to the teenager changes the mood in the room immediately. There is a bonding between teenager and parent, whereas before there was anger and distance. I then ask the mother or father how her or his parents treated the matter, and what feelings were generated from that treatment. From then on, in most cases, the counseling session moves toward resolution.

As you deem it suitable to the age of the child, you can share the more tender and vulnerable events and feelings, such as fear, sadness, hurt, disappointment, frustration, humiliation, anger, shame, embarrassment. You can share thoughts and feelings you may have had as a child, such as running away, escaping, hating, striking out. It is not unusual for a young person to feel hatred and to feel like killing someone when severely humiliated, degraded or threatened. Feelings like these arising from being deeply threatened or humiliated are not signs of some serious trouble within the young person. They are a sign of how highly threatened the youngster is. There is a difference between a spontaneous feeling of hatred or revenge and plans to execute such feelings in action. Making such plans could be a sign of a serious disturbance.

In sharing all this with the growing child, the parent must not do so with a hidden agenda, such as to get the child to behave the way you want, or to like you, or to agree with you. The agenda is to be straightforward, i.e., simply to share your life with its ups and downs so that your offspring can get a more balanced and true picture of you as a human being.

Another thing that can be done is to let the children disagree with you, entering into a civil dialogue much as you would with one of your adult friends. This does not mean you relinquish your authority as parent. But the older the child becomes, the more do the conversations of disagreement take on the modality of discourse between friends.

It is important to check out your personal tolerance of disagreements. Some people have a very low tolerance. These are the ones who have to be surrounded with "yes men." Those who in business and social life are surrounded with those of opposing ideas have a high degree of tolerance for disagreement. How do you rate on a scale of 1 to 10? If you have difficulties with disagreements, then I suspect it will be hard to have a friendly argument with a child or teenager or young adult.

In conversations with children, parents are great inquisitors. "How was school today?," "what did you do at the party last night?" "What kind of a person is Sally?," "how was the football game last night?" "Where are you going?" Parents ask, children reply. In their answers the parents hope to get the kids to share their lives with them. As much as the parents want to have their kids share their own lives, how much do parents want to share their lives with their children? And for the sake of just sharing, not to make a point or teach a lesson! In other words, how much space and time is spent in an average week with the parents sharing their lives with the children? Is it balanced with the time the children are asked to share their lives with the parents?

Another task for parents is to keep a diary or journal. I once had a pregnant woman in my family reconstruction class at the university. At the end of the class she joyously announced that she was beginning a journal that very night in which she was going to record her thoughts and feelings during the pregnancy, birth, and years of her child's growing up. She would then present it to her child when the child was grown and could appreciate the journal.

This student intended to be very honest in the journal, recording the negatives along with the positives. I think that is crucial. There will be no revealing a person's full humanity if only the good side of it is shared. At times, I suspect, it will be difficult for that young mother to put down her true feelings.

I think that keeping a journal will be helpful to the "parlias and parsus" if the journal is used primarily by the author, mother or father, for the sake of the author. That is, if the mother or father journals her or his thoughts and feelings on a daily or weekly basis, dealing with all of life's events, as a way to express himself or herself, reflect, and meditate, then it is done for the benefit of the author.

My wife and I once coguided the reconstruction of a man who had never seen his father. His father had never married his mother because he was already married, even though separated for many years from his legal wife. His Catholicism did not allow him to divorce and enter into a second marriage. The father sent money to support the family from his home in Europe. The father also kept a lively correspondence with this man's mother for many years prior to and after the birth of his son, who was unknown to him. After his mother died, he discovered a large packet of the letters that his father had written. The treasure trove gave him a direct contact with his father and allowed him to know and appreciate how human his father was. This man, with tenderness in his voice, told us that the letters were very romantic and filled with love.

This example illustrates how valuable it is to keep any records, letters, diaries, newspaper articles, or pictures that can be handed over to the grown children later on.

A mother and father might also record on audio tape their reflections and memories of their childhood experiences with their parents and siblings. It would also be important for them to record any information they have about the backgrounds of their parents as well as the stories they heard about their parents.

A variation of this is to interview our parents on video or audio tape about their lives and the lives of our grandparents. Such recordings could then be passed on to our children. Thus four generations of history would be recorded, helping family members understand the human characteristics of their ancestors.

These few ideas should be enough to stimulate your imagination as to how you can help your children see you and other members of their family roots as human.

As the adult children (parlias and parsus) perceive parents as human and begin to relate to them as their equals, the parents (viramecus and winamecas) will be freed of their parenting roles and can be friends with these adults whom they gave birth to and reared.

Chapter Twenty-Two

The Theme of Roots
in Literature

❧

SEVERAL YEARS AGO, a friend of mine ushered me into her office. "Look, Bill, what I've been up to," Jan said. She showed me a large volume filled with photographs, newspaper articles, personal letters, typed stories and accounts, genograms, and chronological lists of family data.

"I've been working on this for five years, and I've finally finished it," she said. "When mother died five years ago I discovered that she had kept all the letters that she had received from me going back forty years. What was amazing, Bill, is that I did not know that she had been keeping these letters, yet on my own I too kept all of the letters she had written to me these last forty years. It was then that I decided to collect all the pictures, articles, records, and letters that I could find or remember and put them together in this book. I connected all the data I found by explanatory descriptions. It's sort of a historical novel."

Jan reproduced the large volume and gave it to all of her living relatives. She made twenty such volumes. When I asked Jan what personal gain she got from doing this, she said, "I feel like I belong to this world. I know that I too will die, and therefore, I live each day to the fullest as I have never done before. I have a legacy to leave besides money."

This simple statement expresses a newfound strength to live

life to the fullest, as well as a new sense of her personal worth. She belongs here, and she is giving something to others. And this was a result of digging deeply into her roots. In her middle fifties, she had grown to the point of maturity that she could appreciate the complex human nature of her parents and family roots.

Jan had produced a book, yet I am sure she would not regard it as a piece of literature. Nevertheless it was her story of her roots given to her family. Her book reflects three simple, fundamental truths, namely, to know who I am depends on knowing my roots, to know fully who I am depends on seeing my root family members as *the humans they really are*, and when *I embrace* this composite picture, I become full, complete, and mature. In view of this, is it any surprise that embracing our roots has been a fundamental theme in literature?

The most explicit example is Alex Haley's *Roots*. In chapter 6, I talked about the TV series based on Haley's book (New York: Dell, 1976). *Roots* is the clearest presentation in modern times of the three truths that my friend Jan encountered. Haley's *Roots* is a literary masterpiece, not just because it presents the historical data of seven generations, but because Haley so well describes the human characteristics of his roots. He casts them in the lively and picturesque context of the day and time.

Toward the end of the book (p. 721), Haley speaks of the process whereby the people in his book became alive for him, no longer merely names with dates. He took all the stories he had heard or read and *used his imagination* to picture them humanly alive.

He writes, "In my mind's eye, rather as if it were mistily being projected on a screen, I began *envisioning* descriptions I had read of how collectively millions of our ancestors had been enslaved... as my own forebear Kunta had been.... I *envisioned* the many dying... and those who made it,... shaved,... often branded with sizzling irons; I *envisioned* them being lashed and dragged.... I *envisioned* them shoved, beaten, jerked down into slave ships... " (emphasis mine).

After years of research in archives and of talking to many people, he finally visited the African village of Juffure to hear the tales of his family from the village *griot* (a person who maintains the oral history of the village and tribe). When he returned home on a freighter, he slept each night in the cargo hold, imaging what it was like to be a slave in chains being taken to a new land, wrenched from one's home and roots.

Haley's journey to see his roots as human filled him with emotion and a sense of destiny that he talks about in the final pages of his work. He writes, "There is an expression called 'the peak experience' — that which emotionally nothing in your life ever transcends. I've had mine, that first day in the back country of black West Africa" (717). He was filled with his roots, completed. From reading these final pages you sense how this journey of many years gave him such a sense of profound satisfaction and fulfillment. I am saddened that he is no longer with us on this plane. I would have liked to have asked him more details about what his going back home did for him, how it added to his own maturing process. In any event, I believe that Alex Haley with his *Roots* has given to America a gift that we will fully appreciate only with the passage of time.

I once had the opportunity to visit with some friends of mine in Chicago, Ed and Carolyn Quattroccki. I was passing through on my way to guide a person's family reconstruction. Ed earned his doctorate in literature from Loyola University in Chicago. For twelve years he was a professor of Renaissance literature at Ohio University in Athens, Ohio. He is now a commodity trader. He claims, though I cannot prove it, that he is the only Shakespearean trading cattle at the Chicago Mercantile Exchange. Carolyn is the mother of five children and the grandmother of four and a former teacher in the field of child development. Here are a few of the relevant pieces of our conversation:

"Ed, are you suggesting that my work may not be original? What do you mean?"

He was slightly taken aback and quickly responded. "First of all, Bill, I think that your effort to help ordinary human beings achieve the self-knowledge that brings peace and harmony in their lives through an examination of their family roots, especially in seeing these people as human through imaginative processes, is exciting and new, but, paradoxically, it is also old, tried, and true.

"Let me point out that when people don't understand their roots, disastrous consequences can result. These are perhaps most graphically portrayed in two of the most widely read and influential books of the past fifty years."

"What books are these?" I asked.

"Aldous Huxley's *Brave New World* and George Orwell's *1984*," Ed replied. "Although these two novels portray different kinds of totalitarian societies, they have one obvious means of control in common. Both totalitarian states consider any human relationship dangerous, especially love among members of the family.

"In Huxley's novel, babies are not born as a result of a loving human relationship; they are decanted in test tubes in a laboratory. The rulers maintain control by a systematic obliteration of the memory of their subjects; Mustapha Mond, the World Controller, puts the central creed very simply, 'History is bunk.'

"And the same theme with variations informs the structure of Orwell's novel. Children are trained to spy on their parents and to inform the Thought Police about any deviation from orthodoxy. For the subjects to have memory of the past is a threat to the security of the state.

"So, Bill, here we have examples of two highly influential pieces of literature expressing the horrors of what happens to humans if they cut themselves off from their past and their roots."

"Okay, Ed, but what I want to know — is there anything in literature that more explicitly supports my theme?"

"Heavens, yes! The reason I'm smiling is that I'm surprised that you don't already know the answer to that!" Ed exclaimed.

"Well, I do know that the theme is portrayed in modern literature, like in Kennedy's novel *Ironweed*. But you're the expert in ancient literature. I want to know about that," I said.

Ed answered, "My expertise is in Western literature, so I can only speak from that point of view. Take the seminal pieces of literature of Greece, Rome, and the Israelites. Here you'll see this great concern for being connected to one's roots.

"The great epic poems of Greece, the *Iliad* and the *Odyssey*, are essentially about families and the search for national identity. Though both the *Iliad*, which focuses on the long Trojan War, and the *Odyssey*, which recounts the twenty years of the travels of Odysseus after the war, are diffused with violence and suffering, they also reveal the great reverence that the Greeks had for their families and their ancestors.

"The episodic plot of the *Odyssey* is knit together by the quest of Odysseus to return home to his wife, Penelope, his son, Telemachus, and his father, Laertes, after the Trojan War. Odysseus encounters innumerable difficulties in returning home, spanning some twenty years. The wily Odysseus endures adversity with heroic courage, mainly because of his faith, hope, and desire to see his family again. The importance of this inspiration for Odysseus is especially significant near the middle of his journey in Books X and XI."

"This is similar to experience of many people I have dealt with in helping them to return to their roots," I said. "They too have difficulties. I have discussed some of these difficulties at the beginning of the book."

Ed continued. "Well, I'm not surprised. A literary classic taps into the most basic human themes and dilemmas. Let me tell you about one of Odysseus's encounters, because it bears so directly with the central theme of your book.

"Odysseus is required to visit the house of Hades to consult with the blind prophet Tiresius. Among the other shades Odysseus speaks with in Hades, the most important, after Tiresius, is his mother, Anticlea. First Tiresius tells Odysseus of the future, that he will endure more terrible tribulations, but that eventually he will arrive home and slay the wooers of his wife, Penelope, and that he will die peacefully in his old age. Then he has a poignant and significant conversation with his dead mother. He asks her to tell him of the conditions at home — how she died, how it goes with his wife and father and son. And she responded with the heart-rending truth that his wife and son remain in his house but they are in great distress, that his poor, old, and feeble father sleeps on the ground in the winter and grieves continually about his lost son, and that she, his mother, died of a broken heart.

"Now, Bill, this has special significance in regard to the theme of your book. *In order for Odysseus to have the courage to go on, he must see the future through the blind eyes of the prophet, Tiresius, and he must see the past and his rootedness in his family by spiritually communing with his mother.* This short episode in the vast, sprawling epic gives reason enough to explain why Homer is one whose art reaches to the summit and why all subsequent poets pay him homage."

"Hmm, yes, I see that. What other significant piece of literature is there that reflects this theme?" I asked.

"Bill, if we move to the Roman culture we find the same in Virgil's *Aeneid*," Ed replied. "His great epic is a synthesis of Homer's

Iliad and *Odyssey;* it is to the Roman language and culture what Homer's epics were to the Greeks. Virgil's hero, Aeneas, is different from Odysseus in many important respects. But what both Odysseus and Aeneas have in common is their deep and abiding allegiance to family and friends. There are many parallels between the adventures of Odysseus and Aeneas, particularly those that relate to the family.

"Aeneas tells the story of the Trojan War and how he managed to escape. As he tells his story in the first three books of the poem, several aspects of his character reveal themselves. He has a great love of country and of family. He is burdened by a painful and loving memory of Troy, but *he gains strength from this memory.* By looking backward at his pain he gains strength to look forward to the founding of Rome.

"In another scene, Aeneas visits his dead father, who occupies an honored place in Hades in the Elysium of the fields of Gladness. Aeneas approaches and sees his father deep in thought: 'telling over / The multitudes of all his descendants, / his heroes fates and fortunes, works and ways.' He reassures Aeneas that although the path ahead will be hard and painful, he will eventually found the kingdoms of Rome and will be the progenitor of a long line of kings.

"The stories of Odysseus and Aeneas have had a pervasive influence on all successive generations in the Western tradition."

"Ed," I said, "I think it significant that Odysseus seemed to see the human qualities of his parents. Odysseus envisioned his father grieving over his apparent loss and his mother dying of a broken heart."

"I agree," Ed said. "It is even reflected in the Bible. The Israelites were very concerned with their roots, as illustrated by how often they use genealogies to convey a sense of who they are. We see this in the book of Genesis.

"But what emphasizes your point about seeing these people as human is found in the genealogy of Jesus. You would certainly think that Matthew would want to paint the best picture of Jesus and the family from which he came. In the beginning of Matthew's Gospel he begins the story with a lengthy genealogy — again to give a sense of who and what Jesus is. Yet we learn that 'Abraham was the father of Isaac, and Isaac the father of Jacob, and Jacob the father of Judah and his brothers, and Judah the father of Perez and Zerah by Tamar being their mother.' Judah, the predominant of the twelve sons of Jacob/Israel, had three other sons by his wife Shua, but these three — Er, Onan, and Shiloh — are not mentioned in the genealogy of Jesus. The two sons mentioned, Perez and Zerah, were begotten out of wedlock by Judah with his daughter-in-law, Tamar.

"Matthew's inclusion of Judah and Tamar and their illegit-imate sons is consistent with what follows in the Gospel. As Matthew makes clear repeatedly, Christ's words and actions re-veal his acceptance and love of all his brothers and sisters, the tax collector as well as the prostitute. Matthew did not whitewash the family background of Jesus.

"So you see, Bill, the seminal pieces of literature from the Greek, Roman, and Hebrew cultures stress the importance of be-ing connected to one's roots or ancestry. It is from being rooted that one draws the inspiration and strength to go forward. These three cultures are the fountainheads of our own Judaic-Christian Western civilization."

"I think what may be new in my book," I said, "is the empha-sis on seeing these people as human so that we can accept the wholeness of these roots — not just to accept them as a father or mother. I know that this has not received much emphasis in psy-chological literature. In the last fifty years the emphasis has been on separating from family in order to live in one's own shoes, as it were. The thrust has been that in order to become individualized you need to break away from the family."

"But isn't that true?" Ed said.

"Yes, but there is more to it than that. And that is what I'm stressing. You need not only to break away, but then you need to return — *not in the old way of being,* but to discover these roots as human."

By this time it was about 11:00 P.M. But Ed, Carolyn, and I felt very awake and energized.

Then Ed spent the rest of the evening telling me the most fasci-nating story of his own trips to Italy and Ireland to visit the places of his ancestors. He took his mother and Carolyn to Ireland where his mother, in her eighties, met her younger brother, whom she had not seen for over sixty years and whom she thought had died. Her younger brother had thought the same of his older sister. As Ed described the meeting I could sense the joy and elation in both

Ed and Carolyn. It was obvious to me that Ed's deepening his connection with his roots was a significant step in his life, and one in which Ed and Carolyn found deeper meaning in each other.

By this time it was two in the morning, and we were ready for bed.

As this theme is central to the seminal literature of our culture, so it is again no surprise to see this theme repeatedly in modern literature. To take but a few examples.

The novel *The Prince of Tides* (New York: Bantam, 1987) is the story of Tom, the protagonist, his twin sister, Savannah, and their older brother, Luke, who struggle to become whole persons. They are raised by complicated parents who offer their children both a body of strengths as well as a reign of terror. The children grow up contending with and escaping from their abusive family history while at the same time trying to accept their roots.

Savannah contends with her background by escaping her roots, moving physically and psychologically from South Carolina to New York. She develops severe mental problems. She regains her health and strength and at the end of the novel is reconciled with her father just released from prison. After a beautiful evening on her father's new shrimp boat, regaling in the evening's dance between the rising moon and the setting sun on a river in South Carolina, she says, "I'm going to make it Tom. . . . Wholeness, Tom. It all comes back. It's all a circle." She has come back to accept her roots, especially her father.

Luke loses his life fighting to maintain his home and land, the soil of his roots. Luke says it very simply, "How do you start over when you can't look back? What happens to a man when he looks back over his shoulder to see where he came from, to see what he is, and all he sees is a sign that says, 'Keep Out'?" (600).

In understanding how his father and mother were raised, Tom finds the way to accept them. Early in the book this theme is announced. "Because I needed to love my mother and father in all their flawed, outrageous humanity, I could not afford to address them directly about the felonies committed against all of us. I could not hold them accountable or indict them for crimes they could not help. They, too, had a history — one that made me forgive their transgressions against their own children. In families there are no crimes beyond forgiveness" (8).

Tom understood how his father "as a child had felt neglected and abandoned and neither of his parents had even laid a hand on him" (182). He understood what it must have been like for his father's mother to have left him for five years at the age of six.

The theme announced on page 8 is repeated near the end of the novel: Tom speaks, "To our surprise, Savannah and I agreed that we had been born to the worst possible parents but we would have it no other way. On Marsh Hen Island while waiting for Luke, I think we began to forgive our parents for being exactly what they were meant to be. We would begin our talks with memories of brutality or treachery and end them by affirming over and over again our troubled but authentic love of Henry and Lila. At last, we were old enough to forgive them for not having been born perfect" (631). (Note how points I have been making in my book are so simply expressed here. Tom refers to his parents not as Father and Mother, but as Henry and Lila, perceiving them as persons equal to him. "At last, we were old enough..." reveals that it takes a certain amount of growing into life's experiences to be able to see one's roots as human so as to be able to "forgive.")

Ironweed by William Kennedy also reveals the power of returning to one's roots. This novel is an excellent example of the special thrust I have been making in this book, namely, the importance of seeing our parents as human rather than in the roles they played. It is not sufficient, in my belief, just to have names, dates, and biographical facts about one's roots — much that a typical family tree contains. Nor is it sufficient to perceive these people as father, mother, grandparent, aunt, or uncle. We need to get behind the behavior of those roles to see the full human person.

Francis Phelan, the central character in *Ironweed*, does just that. He is an alcoholic derelict living on skid row in Albany, N.Y. He has abandoned his wife and children and has not seen them in many years. Toward the end of the novel, Francis decides to pick up a few dollars by working for a rag picker, Rosskam. Rosskam directs his horse and wagon into the old neighborhood in which Francis was raised. As the wagon rumbles through the streets, Francis begins to remember his mother and father and early childhood experiences. As his reflections grow deeper, he begins to see his family differently. His years of experience allow him to see some aspects of his family he had not appreciated before. The ride on Rosskam's wagon affords Francis an opportunity to return to his roots, to see these people more as human than as parents and siblings. He connects to them on an adult-to-adult level within his heart.

After this episode, without any explanation, Francis overcomes his fears and returns to his wife and family for a visit for the first time in years. It is a tentative visit, but one in which he clumsily tries to express his guilt and his love for the family. As the novel ends, the reader is left wondering whether Francis will go back to being a bum or return to his family in a permanent way.

The novel suggests to me that it was in returning to his roots and becoming more appropriately connected to them that Francis garnered the strength to visit Annie, his wife, and his grown children.

Hector Babenco, the Argentine director of the film *Ironweed*, in speaking about the movie said, "When you make a move, you want something, and yet you don't know why.... There is something about the guilt of this character, something about establishing harmony with your past, something about having the courage to come back to the home base of your past and face it."

A novel that speaks to the same point but in an opposite way is *The Death of Jim Loney* by James Welsh. Jim Loney is a native American who struggles with life and can't make it. He is a man cut off from his culture and roots. It is clear from the story that his inability to cope successfully with life is due to this lack of being rooted.

Literature of all cultures stresses the value of being connected to one's roots. Some literature emphasis the theme of developing a new relationship with one's parents and ancestors. The protagonist moves a child-to-parent relationship to an adult-to-adult relationship that envisions the parents as human.

The more I have come to see the essence of the point I have been addressing in this book, the easier it is for me to see the strains of this essence in literature. Twenty years ago I had not detected it.

As I see this in literature I am even more convinced that perceiving the family members of our roots in their humanity rather than in their family roles is a vital and distinct stage of personality development. I think it is the last stage in the maturing process, preparing us to face the final events of our life.

Lao-tzu, who lived about five hundred years before Christ, wrote in the classic *Tao Te Ching:*

Just realize where you come from:
this is the essence of wisdom

Each separate being in the universe
returns to the common source.
Returning to the source is serenity.

(Taken from the translation of Stephen Mitchell, Harper & Row, 1988.)

Chapter Twenty-Three

Facing Death with Peace

✨

I T IS MY OPINION that we will be better able to face death with peace, equanimity, and acceptance if we have reconnected with family roots in the way I have been suggesting in this book.

In order to validate my thesis, I looked for research or studies on this subject. To my surprise, I could not find any. I thought that surely someone would have thought about this and would have made this connection and studied it. But I have come up empty handed. If you, the reader, know of any such studies, please write to me. My address is in the appendix.

I decided to interview people who have had extensive experience with people facing death to see if they noticed any correlation between mature relationships with parents and family roots and the ability to accept death peacefully. I interviewed social workers, hospital chaplains, hospice workers, therapists, and physicians. They were very cooperative and interested in my inquiry. Some of their stories and comments follows.

A chaplain in a large inner city hospital's Hospice Unit had previously spent time assisting patients dying with AIDS. Because she had also participated in a family reconstruction, she knew the difference between relating to one's relatives in terms of the roles they played as grandmother, uncle, mother, or father, and relating to them in terms of shared humanity. She was intrigued with my thesis; "What a juicy and interesting thought," she commented.

In her experience with dying patients she did not find many

who had made this perceptual shift of relating to their parents on an adult-to-adult basis. Many seemed to have some barriers with their parents and continued to deal with them as parents who had failed them in some way.

However, she did notice a correlation between those who had not reconnected with their roots in this way and those who had trouble leaving their own grown children. She told me of a woman in her early forties dying of cancer who had reconciled herself with her father but not with her mother, who had been abusive to her as a child. She fought for her life, trying to overcome the cancer because she "had to live for her daughter." She began to feel differently about her abusive mother. She moved from feeling angry at her to feeling sad and helpless. She still had not gone full circle to see her mother as a human being, but she was on her way. As she began to see her mother differently, she began to feel anxious.

This chaplain didn't know why this anxiety began to appear at the very time the patient began to change her perception of her mother. The chaplain thought that perhaps this perceptual shift was strengthening her so that the patient was able to admit the devastating progress the disease had made in spite of the radiation and chemotherapy. Thus she had to face the fact, unconsciously, that she was going to have to leave her daughter. It would be interesting to know if she was able to let go of her daughter as she completes the reconciliation with her mother.

The chaplain recited another story concerning a woman in her seventies who died of cancer. This woman had had a beautiful relationship with her own parents and husband, who were dead. She also had a fifty-year-old daughter and a twenty-year-old granddaughter, whom she dearly loved. Leaving them behind was troublesome for her. However, as she approached her death, she became very peaceful, blessing her children and grandchildren, giving them to God. Some thirty-six hours before she died she said, "I want to be with my family."

The chaplain would not say conclusively whether the relationship to the woman's own family roots had shifted or not. She did think that the wholesome connection she had with her roots had something to do with her peaceful death. The chaplain said she was the most peaceful person she had ever assisted in dying.

The chaplain said that this woman accepted death as a reality belonging to every human being; she had a relationship with God carrying with it a promise of reconnecting with her family; she reawakened the old desire she had at her husband's death years ago, which was to die and be resurrected with him; she was very generous during her life, making extended families of her friends wherever she went; she lived her values with integrity and therefore had few regrets; she was spiritually "wired," seeing the presence of God around her; she and her family could openly talk about death and her dying.

This hospice chaplain said that the longer she is in this work, the more she sees how mysterious death is. It is as if all of life's mysteries emerge in the act of dying. As a result she is becoming less quick to be sure of statements about the dying process. There are many factors that coalesce into being able to die with peace and acceptance. She was excited about my thesis and felt that being able to accept one's roots as human and thus be connected in an appropriate way with one's family of origin is one of the factors that helps a person to die peacefully.

She went on to say that the physical body doesn't die easily; it wants to live. The spirit may be ready to die, but for some strange reason, the body often fights on. She said that people "die in labor akin to the labor of birth. There is sweat and blood. It's like the labor of birth into the next world."

We discussed this phenomenon of the spirit's willingness to die, but the body's hanging on. We both felt that in such cases there is some unfinished business that the person needs to accomplish before dying. It was as if the person on a conscious level said, "I'm willing to go," but the body, expressing the unconscious, is saying, "Wait, there is still more to do before we go." We both felt the mind-body unity is real.

This chaplain beautifully summed up her work with those dying as "to be with them as they are, to help them name their dying, and to live in it."

Our discussion recalled to me an experience of a friend of mine who died. This person over the years was admired and loved by many friends and working associates. Her parents were long deceased. She had several brothers and sisters, but had unresolved issues with one sibling. In the last weeks of her life, her friends gathered to help and support her in her sickness and dying. About a week before she died, she called in her siblings and said her goodbye to them. She told them they could now return to their homes, as her friends could look after her.

Her family decided not to go home, but they did not return to her bedroom; they simply stayed at the house. In about four days she fell into a coma. Her physician said that there was no reason for her to be alive and he couldn't understand why she had not died. He told this woman's friends that he wanted the family to return to her bedside. Her friends said that she had said her goodbye to them and told them to return to their homes. The physician insisted that the family return to the bedroom.

The siblings returned, stood around the bed in silence, and within five minutes the woman died. Who knows the explanation of this phenomenon? My hunch is that there was something unfinished between her and her siblings, perhaps with the one with whom she had unresolved issues. And that somehow in that final five-minute gathering the business was finished.

I interviewed a family therapist who is also a nurse. She began assisting the dying as a nurse in the Vietnam war. After she came home she continued her help with the dying. She is recognized in her locale as a leader in this endeavor.

I asked her what she noticed about those who were able to die in peace. She said that they were able to go through some sort of a goodbye ritual with their loved ones. They were surrounded by loving and caring people. They had a feeling of fulfillment; they felt they were leaving a legacy behind them. As a result, they had fewer regrets about their lives. They had led worthwhile lives. People tend to die as they live, she said. And she had noticed that the less unfinished business they had, including that with their family of origin, the easier was their dying.

She added that when people were of foreign extraction, playing their folk music and speaking to them in their native tongues was very soothing and comforting.

She said that her comments applied mainly to those who had a slow death. There was time and energy for saying goodbye and to be surrounded by loved ones. There was time to heal wounds.

Those whose death comes suddenly use their energies just to cope with the dying process. Like the hospice chaplain, she noted that dying takes much energy, and in a weakened condition there isn't any energy left over to do anything but tend to the most immediate problems.

I interviewed Ken Hamilton, M.D., who started H.O.P.E. (Healing Of Persons Exceptional) in his home state of Maine. H.O.P.E. sponsors support groups for those with terminal illnesses. Ken has assisted many patients in their dying process. He has observed that many dying people in their last moments envision one or several relatives, such as a mother, father, or husband, who are dead. Their facial expressions indicate that some sort of a dialogue is going on between them. He said that when this happens their face and body relax and they seem to be at peace.

We discussed the idea of being reconciled with members of one's family roots if that was necessary. He saw the enormous importance of achieving reconciliation in order to die in peace. We used the word "reconciliation" while others I talked to used the expression "resolving unfinished business."

He talked about how in the last few years since his mother had died, he has been able to feel greater reconciliation with her through understanding more clearly some human aspect of her that he had not seen before. Seeing her more fully human opened the door for this further reconciliation, which gives him peace.

In my experience the process of reconciliation, forgiveness, compassion, whatever word you want to use, embraces one of two experiences. Either the parent admits his or her error or failures, or the grown daughter or son understands more clearly the deeper or more complex human reality of the parent. One or the other allows a person to be reconciled with one's parent. So it is in changing one's perception of one's parents, from that of seeing them as parents to that of seeing them as human, that enables a person to accept them as part of self. That is reconciliation.

Another case involved a person who was in a fatal car accident in which she and her husband were "killed." In this accident she had an out-of-body experience of being dead and being with her husband and previously deceased mother and father. She felt peace in being with the three of them, but decided that she had more to do on this earth. Her husband decided he wanted to die. She came out of her death experience and regained consciousness. She discovered that she had indeed been in a terrible accident and that her husband was killed. She is still alive and lives with a serene sense of well-being.

This story is similar to that of a man I talked to in a midwestern state who also had what is called a near-death experience. Over nineteen years ago he suddenly collapsed and was sent to the hospital. He had had a grand mal seizure. He has not had one since then and ceased his medication one year after the seizure. After he regained consciousness, he recalled he had had something like an out-of-body experience. As he put it, "I can't remember the transition from life to the spirit world. I remember I 'awoke' to find myself outdoors, and to my right was a high grassy terrace that went up at about forty-five degrees, flattened out, and then went up again to the south. In front of me to the east the terrain was flat. I saw a light like a moon above the horizon and a path that led from where I was to the light. On the path coming toward me there was a being that had a familiar look. On my right came another being that also looked familiar. At the time I did not clearly recognize them, but after I regained consciousness I recognized them as my grandmothers. I remember that my feeling in the experience was one of extreme elation, ecstasy. I've never had that feeling at any time in my life. I was wide-eyed, wanting to experience anything there was — like a kid at a circus.

"They said, 'No, we have to wait here.' I asked why. 'Because they're still working on your body,' they said. I accepted that.

"We sat down; one sat on a tree stump, I sat on a log, the other person kept standing. All of a sudden I had this feeling, 'I have to go back,' but I didn't want to because I'd never felt so good in my life.

"I awoke with a heart specialist over me. He asked me questions to test my memory.

"I've tried not to embellish this with imagination. I have a degree in journalism and know the difference between what is objective and what is imaginative. I can't remember when I first told this experience to anyone. At the hospital I was examined by a psychiatrist who told me that my improvement was nothing short of phenomenal since I had quite a bit of brain damage. Very probably I told him. After that, I told various members of my family."

I asked him about his grandmothers. Both had been dead for many years. He loved them very much and felt that they loved him. I asked him what he made of this experience. He said, "I remembered being immediately impressed with the reality of it. It really happened; I didn't hallucinate. Later, it impressed me that there is a spiritual life as real as our actual life."

I asked him if it made any difference in his daily life. He said that he was always a churchgoer and believed in God. "My awareness changed," he said, "in that I accepted the fact that there is a spiritual life. It made me unafraid of death. Death is a transition. It is God's plan; it is not ours to question, but to accept. I felt better about myself because I was now living with spiritual hope. Years later they found that I had developed lung cancer. I accepted this and was open to dying if that was my fate. If the treatment works, it works. I was not aware of any internal struggle to live. I don't live in fear."

In these near-death experiences, the woman saw her parents and the man his grandmothers. Both the woman and the man had a happy and solid relationship with these people of their roots. I think it significant that these powerful experiences, which allowed these two people to live in peace and not afraid to die, were connected to having a solid relationship with these important people in their families of origin. It further suggests to me that our roots are part of us, and to be appropriately connected to the important relatives in our lives and accepting them as part of us has something to do with our being able to die in peace.

I spoke to the coordinator of a hospice in a large city. She has spent over eight years in assisting people to die. She said that those who left no unfinished business before dying, as a rule, died more peacefully than those who still had not healed personal wounds. In hospice work, if there is time and the patient has the energy, the hospice worker tries to assist the patient in completing unfinished business.

She gave as an example a recent case where a man in his middle fifties was dying and was being cared for by his seventy-six-year-old mother. There was a set of complicated factors in the family system that propelled these two people to be highly dependent on each other. The middle-aged man had never married. He still had a son-parent relationship to his mother, reaching out for her approval of him. But he was also angry at his mother. Perhaps he was angry at not getting her approval; perhaps he was angry at himself for being so dependent and displaced the anger onto her. In any event, this feeling of needing his mother while at the some time being angry at her persisted up to a week before he died.

The something happened. For one thing, his mother was physically and emotionally depleted from the endless caretaking of her son. Perhaps the son noticed this. But, for whatever reason, he suddenly relinquished his need for her approval. He was resigned to her being as she was. While she clung on to him, he let go of her. He freed her from her role of being his support and the one to approve of him. In his last week on earth he was at peace.

The hospice coordinator remarked how paradoxical it is that those who have a secure, loving, supportive, and accepting relationship with family members are better able to let go of them in death. Contrariwise, those with a poor relationship with family members have a difficult time in being free of them.

I think the reason for this paradox is that true love has the quality of accepting others as they are. Thus, the dying person can be accepting of both the fact of dying and leaving the family behind. The family members of the one dying, possessing true love, can accept the person's dying and their being without that person here on earth.

A similar view was expressed by a professor of psychology who has devoted a considerable part of his professional life to the subject of death. He teaches courses and seminars on what he calls death education.

When I explained to him the topic of this chapter he spoke of the literature on widowhood. It is generally accepted that those widowed are better able to deal with the death of the spouse when the marital relationship has been solid. Those widowed have a difficult time in dealing with the death of the spouse when the relationship has been filled with problems. You would think that a person would be relieved when this spouse died since the problematic relationship is now ended. On the contrary, the unfinished business with the spouse creates problems for the one widowed.

He suggested that the same could hold for those who had unfinished business with their parents or family roots. But, he added that there are many factors that coalesce to enable a person to die in peace. Even those who have achieved a healing with their roots or achieved adult-to-adult relationships, would not find this to be of much help if they lived a daily life in denial of their death. People who deny death generally live lives that are filled with unhealthy choices. Those who in their daily life accept the reality of their eventual dying tend to live healthy, mature spiritual lives.

To the degree that completing unfinished business with our parents and achieving an appropriate relationship with our ancestors helps us mature, to that degree it also helps us face our death. He likewise knew of no direct study or research into the topic of this chapter.

All those interviewed were intrigued with the idea that seeing members of one's family as human rather than in the roles they played could add to a person's peaceful death. Many were not surprised that little study has been done about this. They had not thought of the child-parent relationship within the focus I was thinking about it. Several stated that they would be using this focus in the future. They also stated that in death and dying much of the attention is paid to the immediate needs of physical care and pain reduction, especially for those who suddenly become critically ill. Also much of the effort is directed toward helping the family members grieve appropriately.

If my thesis is correct, then one of the things we can do now to prepare for a peaceful death is to begin to let go of Mother and Dad and see them as Helen and Doug.

I close again with the words of Lao-tzu:

> When you realize where you come from,
> you naturally become tolerant,
> disinterested, amused,
> kindhearted as a grandmother,
> dignified as a king.
> Immersed in the wonder of the Tao,
> you can deal with whatever life brings you,
> and when death comes, you are ready.

Chapter Twenty-Four

A Personal Closing Statement

ഇ

MY FATHER, WILLIAM FRANCIS NERIN, called "Bill" by everyone and sometimes referred to as "W.F." since he signed his name W. F. "Bill" Nerin, died over thirty-two years ago. My mother, Corinne, died in 1981, almost ninety-two years old. I was named William Francis Nerin after my father.

My mother called me "Billy" until one day, around the age of seven or eight, I announced that I wanted to be called "Bill." From that day on I was called Bill by my family. I appreciated that. My father called me "Son." I don't know if that was the Irish way or his own father's way, or because he was Bill and my name was the same. Once in a while he called me "Billy," but after my early announcement of my manhood at seven or eight, he called me "Son."

I called Corinne "Mother," never "Mom." I called my father "Daddy" — as did my older brother and sister. My sister, Celeste, called him that till he died. Later, Nor, my brother, called him "W.F." Although he was their stepfather, Celeste and Nor loved him in a way that, as I grew older, I marvelled at. It was a tribute to him that they so loved him.

I kept on calling my father "Daddy" to his face, but I was embarrassed to let others know I still called him that. I feel that tinge of embarrassment even now as I write this. This shows how powerful the names of people are. The words we call people are symbols of profound meaning. Those symbols carry our life's experience with those people, especially our family roots.

My relationship to my father became convoluted while he was alive. I didn't have the knowledge nor skills to know, at the time, how to move the relationship to one that is more adult-to-adult. He became alcoholic and it was up to me to institutionalize him in his later years in the late 1950s. The treatment of alcoholism was not very advanced in those days. It was all very complicated and mostly painful. So while I still called him "Daddy," I was really his caretaker. He was the sick child, as it were, and I the responsible adult. As I grew up I moved from child, to grown son, to caretaker, bypassing the stage of a peer relationship with him.

It was only after his death and my developing knowledge of psychology (later specializing in family therapy and doing my own family reconstruction) that I was able to move toward a peer relationship with him in my heart.

While I still called Corinne "Mother," I believe that in our adult years we had achieved a fairly good adult-to-adult relationship. I think that she would have been open to my calling her "Corinne," even though it would have taken some effort on her part to get comfortable with it. She was a consummate mother. Luckily, she enjoyed other sources of life, like being in the business world, owning dress shops in the St. Louis area. She was also an avowed lover of friends and had an active social life. She was extremely keen of mind and open to new ideas. So she would have seen the sense of being called "Corinne." I think she would have enjoyed telling her friends the rationale behind it.

This is a long introduction to a meditative visualization I have engaged in. The meditation revolves around the use of the powerful symbols of "Daddy" and "Bill." I chose to focus the meditation on my father since I think that I did not achieve as much of an adult relationship with him as I did with my mother. I relate the meditation to you.

I sat in a chair, relaxed, closed my eyes, and visualized my father with me. We talked about calling each other by our first names. He agreed. As we continued talking, both of us slipped once or twice and used "Daddy," or "Son."

I noticed that when I called him "Daddy," my voice was softer and smaller. When I called him "Bill," my voice was assertive and stronger. I even saw myself leaning forward in my chair. I had a different feeling inside. I really felt as big as Bill. I felt equal to him, but not quite. It was hard to maintain the "Bill." I wanted to slip back to "Daddy."

Bill said, "It's hard to imagine you are sixty-six years old. Why, I died just ten years after that age. By sixty-six I had gone through a hell of a lot. It's hard to imagine you having as much experience as I did by sixty-six. But I know you have."

I wasn't satisfied by visualizing only our talking together. It was difficult to maintain the "man-to-man" status.

So in my meditation, I shifted the scene to doing something with him. He loved socializing in taverns. In his youth, and even in the 1930s and 1940s, the neighborhood tavern was a center of men's social life, at least in the neighborhood in which I grew up.

So I went to the tavern with him, doing something with him rather than just talking. It was easier to be man-to-man, Bill-to-Bill. He shouted across the room to me, "Bill come here, I want you to meet someone."

I called to him at times, "Bill, come here, look at this guy, he's doing tricks." In the tavern, we didn't slip once into "Son" and "Daddy." I felt more manly, his equal. We enjoyed being with each other as older and younger friends.

Then I wanted to shift the scene so he could join me in some of my activities. I flashed onto golf and he caddied for me. But that scene didn't last; the bag was too heavy for him, and he didn't really enjoy it much.

So I introduced him to my friends and we played cards. All evening we called each other "Bill." My friends liked him and I liked him in that setting. He treated me and my friends as equals as we did him.

I then wanted to have a disagreement with him, so the scene went back to our home, one-on-one. I remember arguing with him in real life over racial prejudice. He was prejudiced against Negroes, as African-Americans were called in those days. So we talked about the racial issue.

He was terrific. It was hard to get a disagreement going. He said he now knew why I argued with him in the past. It was because I was always for the underdog. Bill said he was too, but he was blinded on the racial question because of the way he was raised in Cincinnati.

Again it was "Bill" and "Bill," more relaxed, with no need to win the argument or have mutual approval. It was like stating our case and letting the chips fall where they might. Back in the one-on-one situation at home, however, it was not as easy to feel the man-to-man relationship as in the tavern and in playing cards.

This meditative visualization was yet another step in achieving a more appropriate relationship with Bill, who once parented me. I do not think I would have progressed as far as I have if it had not been for the previous thinking I have done about him and having done my family reconstruction. In the "Bill-to-Bill" mode of relating, I felt stronger and bigger inside, more like a man. I plan to do more work on this in future meditations, fantasies, and reflections.

Appendix

୭

I WOULD LIKE TO HEAR FROM YOU, the reader, if you want to contact me about questions or reactions to what you have read. You may want to share some experiences of your own, take issue with some of my views, or expand on your own ideas. As I have learned from interviewing people for this book, I would like to learn from you too.

You may want to know how to do your family reconstruction. I know of trained Guides throughout the country to whom I could refer you. You may want to obtain a video of a family reconstruction to see how it actually goes.

If you are a professional you may want to know about the Family Reconstruction Training Institute, which my wife, Anne, and I have created to train Guides for family reconstruction.

If you want advice on how to proceed on the ideas suggested in this book, please write:

William Nerin
11221 35th Ave Ct. NW
Gig Harbor, WA 98332

An example of such sharing comes from my wife, Anne. After she had read the entire book, suggesting grammatical and editorial changes, she said that I should have added a section on collecting family photographs, an activity very important to her. She has over a dozen albums recording the history of the family. I have never been enthusiastic about such collections, yet I believe she is right. Explorers doing their family reconstructions are very proud to show members of the group pictures of all their family members, especially those of grandparents and great grandparents. And it is amazing how group members are keenly interested in looking at these pictures.

Although I say I am not enthusiastic about this, I smile, for hanging on my office wall is a family tree of my paternal and maternal family and family of origin with pictures of each person above each name. I remember assembling this years ago and how proud I was in doing it. I gave a copy of it to my brother and my sister's grown daughter for their Christmas presents. (My sister had died by then.) It was a very special gift for me to give, another way for me to honor my roots and share them with others.

I have noticed over the years that as I grow more and more into an adult-to-adult relationship with my parents and roots, I see different things as I look at these photographs. They are not so much my father and mother as they are a beautiful man and woman with whom I can relate as equals.

To help you understand your parents and relatives more clearly as the human beings they are, I list questions that may be useful to you. Many of these have been stated in the book; bringing them together in one place may be of value.

Questions for Your Mother and Father about Their Early Lives

- where were you born? what were the conditions surrounding your birth, e.g., what kind of house did your parents live in? were you born at home? who was there at the birth? were there any problems?

- what were your father's/mother's reactions to your birth? what expectations did they have about their new baby before you were born?

- were you breast fed? did you have any early illnesses? were you an easy or difficult baby?

- if you had older siblings, what was their reaction to your birth and early development?

- who lived at home in your early years? who came in often to help rear you? what was the attitude of these live-ins and helpers toward you?

- as you grew up what problems did you encounter? what were your happy times? what gave you pain and joy? how did you feel about yourself?

- where did you go to school? how was grade school for you?

- how many friends did you have in your grade school years? how did you play? what were you learning about life and yourself during this time? any sicknesses?

- from birth to the end of grade school, what was your family life like? what did your mother and father do? how did you get along with your siblings? how did your parents treat each of you? the same? differently?

- how did your mother and father relate to each other? how did they express love? how was anger treated? how were problems addressed? what was of prime importance to your father/mother? what do you wish were different about them? what did you like the most about them?

- what contact did you have with your aunts and uncles and cousins?

- what did your mother's/father's parents do? where did they live? what kind of people were your parents' parents? tell me all you know about your parents' parents.

- what kind of relationship did you have with your grandparents?

- after you entered puberty, how did you deal with your sexual development? did anyone tell you about sex? did you have puzzles, questions? could you talk to anyone about sex? what kind of boys or girls were you attracted to? who was your first crush? first date? what were your dating years like?

- in your high school years or teens, what problems did you have? how did you deal with them?

- in your teens, did anything change in regards to your parents?

- when did you first meet Dad/Mom? what were your first impressions? how did the relationship develop? what can you tell me about your dating, engagement, and days prior to the marriage?

- what were you looking for in a spouse? why?

- what were your dreams when you married?

- which dreams came true and which didn't?

- tell me about the early days of your marriage? what problems did you have? how did you play? have fun? what surprises about each other did you have? how did you handle the surprises or problems. If you had those early days of marriage to live over, what would you do differently?

- did your marriage change your relationship to your parents and siblings? in what way?

- from the time of your birth to my birth, what disappointments did you have? what losses? what successes? during this time, when did you ever feel sharply the feelings of sadness? depression? ecstasy? loneliness? humiliation or shame? thrill? pride? embarrassment?

- during this time, what were your most common fears? your most intense fear?

- during this time, what basic needs were not met? which were met? did you feel you got enough affection, understanding, and acceptance from your parents?

- what burden did you feel was most painful to you? what value or benefit did you get growing up that you cherish?

- what did you learn about being a parent? a spouse? what were the most important things you learned about life and yourself when you grew up? what did you learn it meant to be a man/woman?

- what became important rules in your life? which ones would you like to have changed?

- as you look back upon your life, what do you regret? what do you cherish?

These questions could also be addressed to your aunts, uncles, and grandparents if they are still alive.

Questions for Your Mother and Father about Them and You

- how did you view me as a baby? from two to six? from six to twelve? from twelve to eighteen? how did you view me differently from my brothers and sisters?
- what problems did I cause you? what joys did I offer you?
- what did you learn about me as I developed?
- how was I different from your expectations prior to birth?
- how hard or easy was it for you to let me be me?
- how hard or easy was it for you to let me be different from how you wanted me to be? to disagree with you?
- how do you think you have treated your kids? the same as your parents treated you? differently from the way they treated you?

These questions could also be asked of other members of the family.

You could ask how various social events, such as war, poverty, the Depression, job changes, and moves, influenced your relatives.

You could also explore the family as a system, e.g., if a book was written about the family you grew up in, what would be the title? what did the neighbors think of your family? was that accurate?

You could also ask questions about how other social institutions influenced the family or individual members, e.g., how did religion or church influence your family? how did the work your father did influence him? how did being German in descent influence them? how did the army influence him? how did belonging to a minority impact the family?

These questions are starters. They will stimulate other questions of your own. The answers will stimulate further discussion between you and your parents and relatives. Remember the goal is to discover the deeper intricacies of what makes them the humans they are. Can you see them with their personal names more than with their role names as mother, father, grandparents, aunt, uncle?

Good luck and safe journey!